About The Author

GRAHAM CLAY is a 29 year-old writer and photographer from Brighouse, West Yorkshire.

He has followed the fortunes of Bradford for 20 years, and was secretary of the Supporters Club in the late 1980's.

Since 1990 he has worked for League Publications Limited, publishers of *Rugby League Express*, Britain's biggest selling weekly on the sport.

He has covered the game at home and overseas, including tours to Australia, New Zealand, Fiji and France. He has reported for various national newspapers and agencies, including *The Sun*, *The Observer*, *News of the World* and *Sunday Mirror*. He also contributes to *Sports Weekly* and *Super League Magazine* in Australia and occasionally commentates on the game for *BBC GMR* and *Classic Gold*.

This is his second book after being co-author of the best-selling Super League '96 Yearbook.

A qualified Rugby League referee, he spends his spare time officiating in the Pennine League.

RUNNING WITH THE
BULLS

Bradford's Championship Year

GRAHAM CLAY

League Publications Limited

First Published in Great Britain 1997 by
League Publications Limited
Wellington House, Briggate, Brighouse, West Yorkshire, HD6 1DN

Copyright League Publications Limited 1997

ISBN 1 901 347 02

A CIP catalogue record for this book is available from the British Library.

Designed and typeset in 11.5pt Palatino by Graham Clay at League Publications Ltd.
Printed and bound by Redwood Books, Trowbridge, Wiltshire.

CONTENTS

ACKNOWLEDGMENTS

THIS book would have been impossible to produce without the help of everyone connected with the Bradford Bulls club, especially Chris Caisley and Gary Tasker.

But most of all, I thank Matthew Elliott, his staff and all the players for allowing me to share the season with them. During the countless interviews and photographic sessions they always made me feel welcome and have been totally open and honest. It has been a real privilege to witness the inner workings of such a great club.

Also, Martyn Sadler and Tim Butcher at League Publications for believing in the concept enough to publish this book, and allowing me the time to pursue the Bulls literally around the world.

Nigel Askham at the *Bradford Telegraph & Argus* was a much appreciated travel companion and provided invaluable research assistance, as did the *Rugby League Express* and *Super League Week* reporters, especially Tony Hannan and Danny Spencer.

Thanks also to Lionel Parker and Colin Thomas at Redwood Books, who provided expert advice in helping me to design and set this book in readiness for printing.

Most of the pictures are from my own files, but thanks also to Andrew Varley, Simon Wilkinson, Vicky Matthers, Andy Howard and Martin Robson for additional pictures.

INTRODUCTION

IN his book *Notes From a Small Island*, American writer Bill Bryson is scathing of several towns and cities the length and breadth of our shores.

But he reserves special criticism for one particular city he visited in 1994.

"Bradford's role in life is to make every place else in the world look better by comparison, and it does this very well", Bryson writes.

"Nowhere on my trip would I see a city more palpably forlorn. Bradford seemed steeped in a perilous and irreversible decline. What is one to do in Bradford with three hours to kill?"

Anyone who lives or works in Bradford, especially in its Centenary Year, would no doubt relish the chance of giving Bryson a guided tour of the city. I don't live in Bradford (sorry, I hail from Halifax) but I went to school there and spent seven years working in the city. I'm sure I could find something to amuse our American visitor for rather more than three hours.

To his credit, Bryson does concede that there is an occasional oasis in this barren land.

The Alhambra is the most wonderful place to see a pantomime, he admits.

And he agrees the National Museum of Film, Television and Photography has brought a flicker of light to a corner of the city that previously had to rely on the world's most appaling indoor ice-rink for entertainment.

Oh, and you can get a damn good curry of course.

One can only assume his brief visit did not allow time to venture up Manchester Road to Odsal. If he had, how would he have reported his findings, I wonder?

Back in 1994, Bradford Northern, as the club was then still called, had finished runner-up to Wigan in the Stones Bitter Division One. Their average crowd was over 6,000, quite healthy considering previous years.

But Odsal was a depressing place, devoid of charm and character. On one particularly inhospitable evening when Wigan visited for the biggest game of the year before a live television audience, a suddenly descended shroud of thick fog, just ten minutes after the start, meant thousands of disappointed fans had to return to their firesides sooner than expected.

Chairman Chris Caisley, having got so close to Wigan, was immensely disappointed when the following year the club slipped to seventh and average crowds fell alarmingly by over a thousand. It was time for action.

In the months that followed, Caisley guided the club through a remarkable transformation. What was once ridiculed as the worst place on earth to watch a game of Rugby League has become widely acknowledged as THE place to be during Super League's summer months. Fans flock from far and wide to enjoy a fun-filled action-packed family day out, choosing Odsal ahead of a trip to the seaside or theme park.

Now, Caisley enjoys telling of the supporter in Portsmouth who, bitten by the Bulls bug via satellite television, relocated to Skipton, and of the season ticket holders in Cheltenham, Birmingham and Blackpool.

As the average crowd rocketed to over 15,000, many new supporters enjoyed the unique Bulls experience for the first time, an event that rapidly become the envy, not just of other Rugby League clubs, but sporting organisations throughout the country.

There is a Bulls Fan Club in Australia, and visiting Australian Super League officials made sure they took in gameday at Odsal during their stay this summer.

The 1997 season provided Caisley and his Bulls with just reward, as the Championship landed at Odsal for the fist time in sixteen years. It was truly a season to remember!

Who will forget that opening night against Warrington back in March, the thrilling last-ditch victory at Halifax, the incredible 20-match winning run?

But most of all, that great week in August when the title was clinched at Sheffield and the party that followed the homecoming game against Paris.

It was a remarkable year, one that brought tears of joy to even the hard-bitten souls who years ago stood on the old railway sleepers at the speedway pits end of the Odsal ground and vowed never to watch the summer game.

Such a season deserves a written record, and this is my effort at a tribute to the Bulls' wonderful achievements.

I begin by looking back at the events leading up to the 1997 season. The move to adopt the Bulls nickname, the appointment of Australian coach Brian Smith, the tough decision, releasing long serving players, the assembling of a complete new squad and Matthew Elliott's elevation to head coach when Smith quit the club.

The book then relives the key moments as a fascinating season unfolds, following the Bulls' thundering steps on their charge to the Super League title.

And, of course, it details a second successive Wembley trip in the Challenge Cup and follows them down under to the World Club Championships, revealing one or two lighter moments!

It has been an eye opening and thoroughly enjoyable project. The hardest part has been deciding what to leave out. I could have written a separate book on all the Bulls-related off field ventures, but hopefully I have captured the essence of the playing season. The games are of course the centrepiece to a book of this nature, but I have tried not to dwell on each match for too long and have attempted to tell the story through the endeavours of the coaching staff and players.

I trust you will enjoy reliving the season, and hope this book becomes a useful reference tool for fans of all ages for years to come.

GRAHAM CLAY
OCTOBER 1997

1

REARING THE BULLS

I first saw Matthew Elliott at Horsfall Playing Fields, less than a mile from Odsal and a regular training venue for the Bulls, shortly after he arrived in Britain in 1995.

It was an unusually cold and wet evening for mid-July and Elliott, who had only been in the country for a few hours, was hidden beneath a thick fleece coat and baseball cap pulled down tight around his head. He had travelled several weeks ahead of his new boss, Brian Smith, who had still to tie up commitments with St George in the Australian Winfield Cup.

This was his first meeting with the Bradford players. He stood to one side, simply watching Brian Noble putting the squad through a few simple routines. Occasionally, a player would jog across, introduce himself with a shake of hands and exchange a few pleasantries. After half an hour, Noble called the players together and formally presented them to their new assistant coach and, until Smith eventually arrived, head coach.

Elliott immediately offered advice. In that short thirty minutes he had already spotted a flaw in the forwards' defensive technique, pointing out that their stance was too flat-footed. With great animation he demonstrated what they should be doing.

"I never thought of that..." one of the senior players was heard to say to a colleague.

It was the beginning of a very special relationship that Matthew, wife Karen and daughters Mia, Lucy and Clare would forge with the Bradford club, its players and supporters.

Standing in the cold rain that night, no-one could have predicted what was about to unfold. A little over two years later Elliott, having unexpectedly succeeded Smith, would be named Stones Super League

Coach of the Year after guiding his Bulls to a record-breaking championship win before Odsal's biggest crowds in over 50 years.

Elliott was born on Thursday Island off the Queensland coast, but moved to Townsville when he was three years-old. He played his first game of Rugby League when he was five for a local junior side, the Western Athletes, and stayed with them until he was sixteen when he gave up the game for a year to concentrate on finishing his studies.

"I always wanted to be a PE teacher and, though I loved Rugby League, I was a better cricket player at that time. I'd made a couple of state teams and it was my ambition to play for Australia

Matthew Elliott deep in thought during one of his first games in charge of the Bulls.

at cricket. If I couldn't do that, then I wanted to play Rugby League in Sydney. The Brisbane League was well watched, but this was years before the Broncos came onto the scene and if you were serious about making it as a League player you had to go to Sydney.

"I was an Eastern Suburbs supporter because that was where my Dad played. He grew up in Paddington in the inner city and I just followed his lead and decided that was what I wanted to do.

"I went to college at Lismore, which is now the Southern Cross University, to study sports science. I was 17 and played a bit of country football but that first year was disjointed because I was homesick and travelled back to Queensland a fair bit.

"The next two years were more successful. I told everyone I was older than I actually was because I wanted to play open age and not under 18's. I joined West Austonville in group one of the country league and played two years as first-grade loose forward. It helped me pay my way through university and I played some good football. I really enjoyed that time. I made a couple of representative teams and played in the country championships. They were good times."

His form didn't go unnoticed by Sydney's talent spotters, and an offer was tabled by North Sydney.

"I was caught up in all the things that university life offers teenagers, and I decided against joining them. It's not a regret but, with hindsight, it would have been nice to take that opportunity."

Elliott did eventually go to Sydney, but not to play Rugby League. After graduating he landed a job working in the city council's recreation department. Away from the office, he took up cricket again.

"It was club level just below the Sheffield Shield, and that first year was great. It was the old Sydney club's last year before the competition expanded out towards Hawksbury and Campbelltown. One of the inner city clubs had to go and unfortunately it was my club. I moved out to Randwick and that's when I realised I liked Rugby League people better than cricket people. They seemed more concerned about how you put zinc cream on your nose or how big your kit bag was rather than enjoying the game.

"I got back into playing Rugby League in 1986 when a guy I played cricket with took me down to Bondi United. It went well and I ended up playing half a season with Eastern Suburbs under 21's and even picked up a couple of reserve-grade games.

"The following year I left Bondi to play the whole season with Easts in the under 23's and the reserve-grade. I managed to break through to first-grade once for a bench spot but it was in the days when the Easts club was a transit lounge. Arthur Beetson was the coach and they had paid a lot of money out for big name players but weren't getting the results they expected. A lot of players came and went.

"I wasn't full time but most Sydney players spent as much time training then as they do now. The money certainly wasn't good enough to make a living out of. The first contract I got from Easts was just $4,000. I'll be honest and say it wasn't the best time of my life as far as playing the game was concerned. Easts were a funny club. They bought players rather than developing their own juniors and other clubs didn't like that."

The following year, 1987, was a good one for Easts. They finished third with a team that included Hugh McGahan, but Elliott was ready to leave.

"It just wasn't a good club to be at, although I admired Arthur Beetson who was a good skills coach. He had his critics but he was the only member of the coaching staff I'd have anything good to say about."

Like most Australians, Elliott had a burning desire to see Europe, and decided to quit Easts in favour of travelling the world.

"I was especially keen to come to England and I'd actually agreed to join the old Fulham club. I didn't have a clue about the structure of the game in England and, about a week before I was due to fly, Tas Baitieri contacted me and offered me a start with Le Pontet in France. I told him

I'd prefer to go to England, but he persuaded me with a better financial package than Fulham could offer. I had eighteen months there and had a great time. We won the cup and championship and were twelve points cleat at the top when I left half way through my second season.

"I left because I still wanted to see Europe, and spent the next three months travelling around. Karen came with me and it was a really enjoyable time. She got a job working at a pub in London for a while but we went back home when she got pregnant."

There was another reason for Elliott going back. Whilst at Le Pontet he had played against the touring Australian club side, Penrith Panthers. The Panthers coach was Ron Willey - who, ironically, was later briefly to become Bradford coach - and he was impressed with Elliott.

"They had a guy called Ross Gigg, the football manager. After the game I met him and he asked if I wanted to come back to play for Penrith. Being naive and full of confidence because I was playing well I took that as an offer, so went back and showed up on the training field. After a while I was told there was a trial match coming up and I had to play in it. Nothing was guaranteed. Well, I thought about it and decided I didn't really want to live in Penrith. I had a nice place at Randwick so I didn't bother going to the trial. I told myself I'd get a game somewhere, even if it was just park footy on a Saturday afternoon."

But Elliott's stuttering career took another upward swing when George Morocco, a former Cronulla player who had played against him in France, fixed him up with a trial at St George.

"It was 1989, two years before Brian Smith came back from Hull. The coach was Craig Young and he offered me a deal. We weren't too successful at first. We certainly weren't the most disciplined club, nor the most professional. We spent a lot of time training but the content wasn't much good. We'd start training at six in the morning for a couple of hours, go to work for nine hours and then have another session in the evening. It was tough on Karen because all I ever did was train, work and sleep. I'd go home both mentally and physically exhausted and would just collapse into a deep sleep. Being a player brought some good things though. We had a close network of friends thanks to the club. It was a great club to be involved with, right through from the administration to the top players. Everyone was looked after really well. I still look at it as my club, and I don't know how I'd feel if I ever had to coach against them. It's probably unlikely, but if the opportunity ever came up to coach them I'd jump at it."

Altogether, Elliott played just over a hundred first-grade games for Easts and St George. The highlight, without doubt, was the 1992 Grand Final against Brisbane.

Matthew Elliott during his playing days for St George
in the 1992 Grand Final against Brisbane Broncos.

"My initial feeling on that day was of personal disappointment that I didn't get to play a bigger part in the game. I'd played all the rounds leading up to the semi-final and then got a thigh injury. It was so competitive that once you got an injury you were on the outer and someone else came in to take your place. You just couldn't afford to get injured.

"It had been the best finish to a season I'd ever had, so to end up playing just twenty minutes of the Grand Final was disappointing. But it was still a great experience. I wasn't very well known as a player and after the game someone who had been listening on the radio told me that the commentators couldn't work out who I was so they decided I must have won the Friday night raffle at the club. Two cooked chucks, a leg of lamb and fifteen minutes off the bench!

"But putting those selfish feelings aside, it was great to be involved. I had a heart rending moment on the way to the final when we played Newcastle and Greg McCallum sin-binned me with nine minutes to go. Quite unjustifiably I might add. John Schuster made a break, I got across to tackle him and McCallum reckoned I held him down. We were winning 3-2 when I left the field and I was sure I'd cost us the game. I was convinced Schuster would pop over the penalty because it was only 40 metres out, but amazingly he decided to run it. It was the longest nine minutes of my life!

"The following year I was doubly determined. I'd had the best off-season of all time, was at the right weight, had trained hard and played in all the warm-up games. I was really happy with my form going into that year.

"But when Brian named the team for the first game at Canberra I'd been left out. I was devastated. It was one of those where he had circled me for about three days before moving in for the kill. The way it worked at that time was that two of the subs were fresh and two were picked from the reserve-grade game earlier in the day. I'd always been a reserve but I had a great deal of versatility and thought I'd earned an automatic bench spot. Anyway, I had to start in the reserves against Canberra and coming up to half-time was going well enough to have earned one of those two remaining bench places. Then it all went horribly wrong. In the 37th minute I did everything you could do to a knee. Cruciates, ligaments, the whole lot. It was the first game of the new season but it was my last. It outed me for the entire year.

"I'd been playing on one leg as it was because I'd had a blown left knee for some time. The doctor at St George said I should retire. He said I'd never get back to the player I was, and I have to admit I was never a great player anyway!

"I was only 28 and I didn't want to accept it at first. I tried to come back a couple of times with an eye on the play-offs but broke down each time. Eventually Brian put me out of my misery and said I wasn't going to play first-grade again but he wanted to use me on the coaching side.

"Two weeks before the 1993 Grand Final he offered me a position. I wasn't sure and I had a couple of offers on the table from Souths and Wests but realistically I knew I had to accept I was never going to make it back as a player. Coaching was what I had wanted to do eventually, so I figured it was as good a time as any to make a start. I accepted Brian's offer and took on the under 21's and a development officer role"

Elliott quit his job in local government, where he had gained promotion to Director of Community Services.

"I hadn't a clue how I ended up doing that job. I think the exposure I got from being a Rugby League player helped me climb the ladder quicker than I should have and. though it was a well paid job with a big staff under me, it's not something I would want to go back to.

"Going on the coaching staff at St George meant I had to take a big pay cut from my player earnings, plus I lost my day job salary. It was tough at the time but I knew it was a gamble I had to take. If I hadn't I would have ended up stuck behind a desk and my Rugby League career would have finished for good.

"I don't regret any of it. I was immediately part of the first-grade set-up, with particular responsibility for coaching the front-row. The following year I was full-time assistant to Brian at first-grade level."

"Then came the ARL-Super League split and things turned nasty. It was a sad time for the club because it looked like we were going to merge with Eastern Suburbs, who had become Sydney City Roosters. Their coach was Phil Gould and, though they guaranteed me a job, they couldn't say whether it would be on the coaching side or stuck away in an office somewhere. I was pretty down about the whole thing.

"I walked into Brian's office to

Bulls General manager Gary Tasker headed up the entertainment packages that added a new dimension to gameday.

Brian Smith pictured on his first day at Odsal in the autumn of 1995.

have a moan, and he said shut the door, something's happening. He told me he'd had enough too and was going to quit to join Bradford. He asked if I wanted to go with him as his assistant.

"I was flattered but said I needed time to think. I was reluctant at first. Brian had also asked another member of his staff, David Boyle, but he said no. In the end it all happened quickly. I thought about it, was excited, and went for it."

Two weeks later, on that wet July night, Elliott walked onto Horsfall Playing Fields. It would be another eighteen months before he took charge of a first-grade side, and during that time a host of interconnecting events would lock themselves together to create the biggest rugby club in Europe. The first of those events, and the catalyst for everything that followed, took place in April 1995.

Chris Caisley, Chairman of Bradford since 1989, had lost patience with the lack of progress being made both by his club and the game as a whole. He decided it was time to change Northern's dowdy image and sat down with company secretary Gary Tasker to draw up far-reaching proposals that would rock the very foundations of the proud club.

Tasker had been with the club since 1981. He played for the now defunct Colts side in the days before Academy teams were introduced, but quickly realised he was better suited to a career in administration. He moved into the small single office occupied by secretary Barbara

Winter to look after the weekly 'Odsal Topper" lottery. His appointment doubled the full-time staff!

By 1995, Tasker was company secretary, the most senior member of the off-field operation.

Tasker recalled how it all happened.

"We initiated a five-year marketing-led plan in April 1995. We decided something radical had to happen. We knew what we wanted, and that was an average of 20,000 people at every game watching a winning side and having a fantastic time. We set that target on day one.

"I walked into the boardroom with a picture of a Bull and a few sketchings of different ideas for logos. At that time we had a boar as the mascot, which had historical links with the city, but we needed a vibrant new image. Together, we decided that night to adopt the new name and logo."

It was a monumental decision, and one that created uproar amongst the traditionalists. But it was eased when several days later came the announcement of the switch to a summer season and the creation of Super League.

"Super League came along right on cue. It was just what we needed, because by then we had already made the decision to introduce the Bulls brand. The switch to summer and the Sky deal were coincidental, but fantastic for us."

The newly named Bulls quickly developed both on and off the field, with the much celebrated arrival of Brian Smith.

"I went to see Brian Smith in the May," remembered Caisley. "We had several meetings during the eleven days I was in Sydney and I explained what our plans were for the Bulls. I told him we had decided to change our name and went through our ideas for the future. I outlined what our concept was for Super League in terms of gathering a new audience and creating an entertainment event that would make the club a major force. He was impressed.

"We had a couple of other possibilities but within a few minutes of meeting Brian I knew he was the man for the job. We went for dinner at a restaurant in Botany

Bulls chairman Chris Caisley

Bay and talked through a deal. I was very impressed with his attitude and coaching philosophy. I left him with an offer, came home and finalised the deal over the telephone a few days later.

"He liked what he had heard from us and at the same time was fed up with the in-fighting between the ARL and Super League. We offered an escape from that and a chance to build a whole new team."

Caisley's next priority was to find someone to head up the newly created marketing department. Smith had forged a close friendship with Peter Deakin during the early eighties when he was coach of the touring James Cook High School side and Deakin was heavily involved in the British Upper Schools organisation. The pair shared the same ideals for the game's future and when Smith returned in 1987 to coach Hull their friendship developed further.

"Brian Smith suggested that Peter would be an ideal man to help implement the strategy that we had already decided on. We met him at the end of May and the board appointed him as marketing manager.

"In June we held a major press conference to announce the appointment of Smith and launch the new name and logo. At that time we still had a small administration working out of just one office, so we obtained new office space and began to revamp things behind the scenes."

Contractual commitments to St George meant Smith wouldn't arrive for another five months, but being 12,000 miles away didn't stop him making his presence felt. He began an immediate assessment of the Bulls' playing and backroom staff via reams of fax paper and countless video tapes. One of his first moves was to sack Nigel Stephenson and Neil Holding, who had been assistants to former coach Peter Fox. In their place came Elliott, Smith's number two at St George. He quit the Sydney club and headed for Bradford to be Smith's eyes and ears. Every player was presented with a personal letter, detailing what the new coaching team perceived to be that player's strengths and weaknesses and how they could improve. Nutritional advice and details of individual training programmes followed. For most of the players, still part-timers, it was bewildering and before long the exit signs loomed on the horizon.

"We will be changing a lot of structural things," said Elliott on his arrival. "These changes need to happen, the question is at what speed they will be allowed to happen. It's fairly obvious that by making the changes the club has done so far, Chris Caisley and his Board are looking to be successful, and that means winning championships and trophies.

"We won't implement the Wigan model or the St George model. Whatever changes we make have to be right for the Bradford club, and

The rebuilding process gathered momentum with the arrival
of Bernard Dwyer, Sonny Nickle and Paul Loughlin from St Helens

to be honest it will take most of this Centenary Season to make those
changes. The fans want to see the team winning now rather than later
but that doesn't put us under any pressure. It adds to the challenge but
I'm sure from what I've seen so far that we are heading in the right
direction and have made the right moves on the marketing side, which
these days is totally intertwined with the football side."

When Smith eventually arrived, the Centenary Season was up and
running and the Bulls were struggling before crowds of less than four
thousand. To outsiders, the glitzy launch during the summer of the new
Bulls title and logo didn't appear to have worked. But Smith's immediate
concerns were off the field and, in the role of chief executive rather than
coach, he began the task of revamping the club's administration.

Much of his time in those early weeks was taken up by their star
centre, Paul Newlove, demanding a move. A Great Britain international,
Newlove was the darling of the Odsal crowd but was fiercely loyal to his
mentor Peter Fox. Newlove had been critical of the Board's decision to
sack Fox, and Smith's appointment did little to calm him. Leeds, Wigan
and St Helens hovered around Odsal for weeks, all desperate to claim
his undoubted talent.

Leeds were the first to make an official approach, but Caisley
responded by asking for their world class New Zealand centre Kevin Iro
in return. That quickly ended any Headingley interest and opened the

The Bulls became the best supported club in the first Super League season.

door for Saints. They moved in with an offer of £250,000 cash plus forwards Sonny Nickle and Bernard Dwyer and centre Paul Loughlin.

Everybody seemed happy with the transaction apart from the three players. The trio were visibly shocked and upset at being forced into the move when they were paraded before the media, but the deal provided Smith with an opportunity to totally rebuild the side.

In the months that followed, old favourites such as Deryck Fox, Roy Powell, Neil Summers and Roger Simpson all departed to be replaced by Paul Cook, Nathan Graham, Simon Knox and Matt Calland. Smith also went to Australia to sign Graeme Bradley and Jeremy Donougher. As the season ended the birth of Super League followed, and with it another offloading of players, replaced with a new batch including Steve McNamara and James Lowes. In total, there were 23 new signings in less than a year.

"We used the Centenary Season to build up and get the structure right so we could hit the start of Super League with a big bang," recalled Caisley. "Sure we developed our playing side, but off the field we also made massive strides in administration and marketing."

The upheaval brought reward in the shape of the club's first Wembley appearance in 23 years, going down 40-32 to St Helens in what many described as the best-ever Challenge Cup Final.

Behind the scenes things were also starting to move.

"We developed an administration of 30 staff across eight departments," recalled Tasker.

"Together with the playing staff, that's 100 people totally focussed and committed. Our motto is TEAM - Together Everyone Achieves More. Nothing has been done by chance. People keep saying how lucky we were because we got to Wembley, but luck had nothing to do with it.

"We had an enterprising board willing to invest in the future, combined with good ideas and a lot of commitment."

Tasker, by now General Manager, headed up the creation of what became the Bulls' trademark - a great family day out.

"We brought in expertise with Engine Room Productions. We then reinvested £150,000 a year of News Corporation's money into marketing and pre-match entertainment. We haven't given it all to players, or paid debts off. I'll be honest and say we could have just paid our debts, but we like to think we have speculated to generate more income to create a long term, financially stable future, rather than going for the quick fix. That has allowed us to create something very special on a match day, that in turn has allowed us to open up the whole marketplace.

"We feel that the West Yorkshire area is fairly and squarely up for grabs. We don't think other clubs realise how important it is to have a Community Services department. It is vital to what we are doing, and reinforces the message.

"Our Community Services department, led by Darrall Shelford, Andy Harland and Steve Fairhurst, utilise ten apprentices to assist them in going out to deliver a major programme hitting between 700 and a thousand schoolchildren a week. That dovetails with other initiatives, such as the Classroom in the Park, and the Bulls Roadshow that goes out to trade fairs, galas and agricultural shows. We even have a school for the junior Bullettes that has over 200 girls enrolled attending dance classes each week. It embraces the whole community and creates a phenomenal force. Everyone wants to be part of it. Friends, relatives and workmates get sucked in."

The end of the 1996 season saw the Bulls third in the table and top of the attendance charts with an average of over 10,000. In a remarkable twelve months, the club had established themselves as the leaders in pre-match entertainment and an emerging force on the field.

Critics said they were poaching other clubs' fans by giving away hundreds of free tickets, but Tasker dismissed the allegation.

"We set our strategy and decided which areas we wanted to target. We worked those areas, and papered the market with subsidised incentives to get people to give it a go.

"But they don't run forever. We are converting people all the time and getting them to upgrade. The first upgrade is to full-time fans, and the next upgrade is to being season ticket holders. By then they're Bulls mad, and the next upgrade is buying into the merchandising. It's all about

Chris Caisley manages a smile as Brian Smith announces
he is quitting the Bulls to return to Australia

brand loyalty, and once we have them on board we push out and target another area."

But the success of 1996 was tempered when Smith delivered a potentially massive blow. After weeks of speculation, he confirmed he was to quit to take up a position with Parramatta despite more than a year remaining on his Bradford contract. He announced his decision before a packed Saturday morning press conference at the Forte Crest Brighouse hotel.

"I feel sad to be leaving Odsal so soon," Smith announced. "I had no intention of this happening but sometimes professional opportunities present themselves unexpectedly. Parramatta is a club with great traditions and enormous potential.

"I won't be approaching any of the Bradford staff to come with me, and I hope that for the rest of this season we will have a continuing crescendo of success at Odsal."

Caisley was diplomatic at losing the man he had fought so hard to attract barely a year earlier.

"We understand Brian's position and he understands ours. The club's success will continue. We have only scratched the surface this year and in a few years we will be the biggest club in the game."

The vacant position was one of the most sought after in the game throughout the world. After losing three of the opening five games, the Bulls had lost just once since Wembley and the squad Smith had assembled was regarded as the strongest in the League and held much expectation for the 1997 season. Off the field, they had a new training facility and swimming pool. The reserve team had won their competition, and the club's profile was at an all-time high.

Caisley surprised a few people by instantly ruling out a British appointment, dismissing potential candidates such as Phil Larder, Andy Goodway, John Kear, Andy Gregory and Ellery Hanley. That left a clutch of Australians eager to get their name linked with the job, and the newspapers suggested John Monie, Graham Lowe and Rod Reddy.

As the weeks progressed, it became obvious the appointment was going to be from within and Elliott was touted as the new head coach. He was increasingly involved at press conferences and become the public face of the Bulls in the local press as Smith eased himself out of the job. Eventually, Caisley confirmed Elliott was to be the new chief Bull.

"We wanted to maintain continuity and Matthew came with Brian's recommendation," explained Caisley. "He was considered with others from outside the club, but once we met with him and listened to his presentation about his views and how he would run the operation it was clear that he was his own man and had his own ideas. He impressed us and we felt he deserved a chance. The hardest decision was deciding how long to contract him for. He was untried as a head coach but we decided it would be unfair to give him anything less than two years. He accepted and we left him with freedom of choice in appointing his backroom team."

Had Elliott not landed the job, or indeed had Smith declined the Parramatta opportunity, Elliott now admits he would have packed his bags and left Odsal.

"I knew for a few weeks before it became public that Brian was going to Parramatta. It was a job he had always talked about, even when he was at St George. When he finally got it we both knew I had outgrown the assistant role. If Brian had stayed I would have probably looked for a head coach position somewhere else, but equally if Bradford hadn't given me his job I would have moved on.

"You have to remember that I was already doing most of the coaching because Brian had a horrendous workload off the field in his dual role as chief executive as well as head coach. He was responsible for the off-field staff, but his ambition was still in coaching and when Parramatta came along he couldn't resist the temptation."

Elliott's first task was to appoint his assistant, and it came down to a choice of two. One was Brian Smith's younger brother Tony, who had just finished a playing and coaching role at Workington Town.

But he plumped for Michael Potter, his former playing mate at St George who was with Perth Reds. Potter won two Dally M Medals as the Winfield Cup's Player of the Year, and reached State of Origin at representative level. Only untimely injuries, including two broken ankles, prevented him from playing for Australia and developing into the first choice Kangaroos fullback.

"He had a huge influence on me as a player and they don't come any more uncompromising as a character," explained Elliott. I needed to build up my coaching staff and I also went for Brian Noble because I believe he has unique qualities as a coach. But Michael offered something different too. He's the type who always gets straight to the point and is honest and upfront. He had also played under a wide variety of coaches, men like Warren Ryan, Peter Mulholland, Ted Glossop, Craig Young and Brian Smith. He's benefited from those different styles and, as an inexperienced coach, I needed that quality."

The trio work well together, and have developed alongside each other. Having spent several years as an assistant himself, Elliott appreciates the input from Potter and Noble.

"They have a rapport with the players that I don't have any more. It's funny, when I was out on the training field as an assistant I noticed that when Brian walked onto the field the players immediately started doing things that bit quicker and more purposefully. Now I see that when I walk onto the pitch. It's all down to people's perception of power. I'm the same guy that they were all having a laugh with last year but because I'm now head coach there is that bit of distance between us.

"If I'm honest, I prefer playing to coaching. That's strange because as a player I always wanted to be a coach. I always said this job wouldn't change me. I'd been in positions of responsibility and hiring and firing people before in my day job, but it didn't have the same effect on me as this job does.

"I enjoy being a coach but I'm no longer part of that special community that the players have. It's a bit like being a player who gets dropped. Suddenly you're out of the immediate circle and being part of that circle is a special thing, particularly when it's a successful group of people."

2

UP AND RUNNING

AS the 1997 season dawned, there was a massive sense of anticipation that this was to be the year of the Bulls.

When nearly 8,000 turned up at Odsal on a cold February afternoon for a pre-season friendly against neighbours Keighley Cougars, it confirmed the remarkable transition of the club in barely twenty months.

Matthew Elliott had been head coach for nearly six months, but had yet to take charge of a gameday. In the days leading up to the Keighley match, he took time out to reflect on just how much had been achieved.

"I have to admit I knew nothing about Bradford when I arrived. Brian told me to get over as quick as I could and check out the players and facilities. We watched a few videos together before I left and, by the time I arrived, I had a fair idea of the quality of players. Brian wanted me to set up the new systems in advance of him arriving. I brought a whole new philosophy and started from scratch by teaching players how to tackle, how to pass, how to catch a ball. We really went that far with them. They had been used to training for a couple of hours two evenings a week, but I was there every day and the demands on their time and commitment became much greater. I got a positive response from guys like Paul Dixon, Roy Powell, Karl Fairbank, guys who had achieved a lot in the game and suddenly had this Aussie who was the same age as them telling them that what they were doing was wrong.

"The office staff, too, found it amusing at first that I was at Odsal every morning before them. They thought it was bizarre that I was around when the team wasn't.

Elliott vividly remembers his first look at Odsal.

"When I first walked into Odsal I have to say I was shocked. I was used to a Leagues Club at St George that looked out over a golf course and had every facility a modern player could wish for. At Odsal there

The Bulls added to their growing sponsorship portfolio at the beginning of the season.
JWE Foneshop become associate sponsor, and launched an exclusive 'Bullphone'

wasn't a training facility or a even a gym. I remember asking to have a look at the gym and was shown a small dark room with a heap of junk in it. I took one look through the door and never stepped foot in the place again. It amazed me that a club the size of Bradford, who had enjoyed some success, had such poor facilities.

"There was a lot to be done but fortunately Chris Caisley and the board realised that, and I set out to improve the situation. Gary Tasker and Peter Deakin were friendly faces who fully understood what I had to do and ensured everyone was focussed on going forward with me."

Move forward they certainly did, at a very fast rate of knots. Most clubs could only dream about 8,000 crowds for their most important games, let alone one that was effectively a training session dissected into four quarters with unlimited substitutes.

But the game had purpose. It offered the Cougars a rare opportunity to embarrass their local rivals, and there was some silverware up for grabs in the Joe Phillips Memorial Trophy, played for over the years against a number of clubs as a pre-season reminder of the great New Zealand fullback who joined Bradford in 1950. Phillips played 232 games and amassed nearly 1500 points before leaving to become coach at Keighley.

It was the Bulls' only run out prior to the Challenge Cup, and provided the only opportunity for players to clinch their place in the starting line-up for the new season. Robbie Paul and Stuart Spruce were missing, on duty for their respective countries in the World Nines at Townsville, Queensland, but Matthew Elliott used 20 players as he tested his options in his first game as head coach.

Neither team fully stamped their authority, but the seven tries the Bulls managed during the middle two quarters were enough to outscore the four Keighley grabbed in the first and final sector.

"It's been a long off-season and it was good to get playing again, especially for me because I was on debut as head coach," said Elliott after the 36-10 victory.

"Overall, I'm reasonably happy. There were no real surprises. I expected us to be a little ring-rusty and consequently Keighley got away on us a little bit. I was happier with quarters two and three when there were flashes from each individual that showed our off-season physical regime has worked really well. We looked strong and, when we decided to put things on, Keighley struggled to handle us.

"I was really disappointed with the last quarter. I know I set the players a big challenge by making so many changes and trying different combinations. It wasn't the execution of the plays I was disappointed with but I thought we were easily distracted in that last quarter and we lost our way badly. Perhaps we weren't really on top of our game today but it's hard to expect too much from a pre-season friendly."

Elliott had signed three new overseas players during the off-season. Michael Potter's connections at Perth had alerted him to the availability of Tahi Reihana, a short, stocky but immensely powerful prop forward. He also snapped up the former Gold Coast and Queensland Crushers centre Danny Peacock, a vastly under-rated player who had suffered from not being at one of the more glamourous Australian clubs but who had still managed to earn State of Origin recognition. Ironically, Elliott clinched a two-year deal with Peacock ahead of his old mate Brian Smith, who thought he had secured him for Parramatta and was furious to learn of his decision to head for Odsal.

Elliott's third signing was a young but promising second row forward from North Queensland Cowboys, Michael Hogue.

"It was funny, every player I went after it seemed I was either five minutes ahead or five minutes behind Parramatta. Brian and I were chasing each other around for a while.

"Tahi Reihana had an unfortunate day in that he was concussed after fifteen minutes. He looked OK early on, and showed he's a strong go-forward type of player.

"I was really happy with Danny Peacock. Having played against him myself back in Australia, I know what a good player he is. He brings a lot of quality to our side. He hits hard into a small hole, he's not afraid of contact and defensively he's outstanding. He's also a very strong support player and he seems stronger and fitter than he's ever been, which is very encouraging for us. He's an elite player.

"But the player I was especially pleased with was Michael Hogue. He's only been here a few days and I haven't had a great opportunity to work with him. Before today I had only seen him on video but I was very impressed with him. He gave us a little bit of hit in the middle and carried the ball strongly as well. I was really pleased for him."

(Ironically, Hogue played no further part in the Bulls story and, after the arrival of prop Jeff Wittenberg from Australia, was released to join Paris Saint-Germain).

Elliott also used the game to introduce Warren Jowitt off the bench, another young player with outstanding potential. With the start of the Challenge Cup just two weeks away, and the Bradford fans expectant of another trip to the twin towers, Elliott left the ground to ponder his selection for his first meaningful game.

"Before today's game there were one or two spots available that I had to have a look at, plus there were the new guys," he said. "It was a friendly and everyone had an opportunity, but I'm pretty close now. I know how things are going to go in the short term, and when Matt Calland's back in another month and fully fit it will be hard to keep him out of the first team."

Two weeks later, the Bulls set out on the Wembley trail in devastating style, crushing second division Hunslet Hawks. Peacock crowned an impressive debut, scoring two tries and landing the man of the match award in a performance that made him an instant crowd favourite.

Elliott decided against playing Stuart Spruce and Robbie Paul who were still suffering jet lag after their long flight back from Australia, but he erred on the side of caution and had them on the bench just in case Hunslet threatened to cause an upset.

Their absence allowed Nathan Graham to start at fullback and Graeme Bradley moved up to halfback to create a centre berth for Peacock's debut.

By half-time the Bulls had rattled up 40 points without reply. They totally steamrollered the Hawks, with the midfield triangle of Bradley, Glen Tomlinson and Steve McNamara spraying the ball out to the wide runners who continually made inroads into a fragile Hawks defence.

Danny Peacock on his Bulls debut in the pre-season
Joe Phillips Memorial Trophy game against Keighley Cougars.

The Hawks offered a little more resistance after the break but it degen-
erated into a scrappy half strewn with penalties, scuffles and yellow
cards. Bradley departed to the sin bin after a long verbal tussle with
referee Karl Kirkpatrick and there was an all-in brawl following a
confrontation between James Lowes and Simon Tuffs.

Tomlinson was also yellow carded after a scuffle in the Hawks' in-goal
area, and there was more trouble after Brian McDermott's 71st minute
try which posted the half-century.

At the end of 80 minutes, the Bulls had posted a 62-10 win and the
following day they went into the fifth round draw. They were eager for
a home game, but got the draw no-one wanted - a tough trip to much-
fancied London Broncos.

It meant a quick return to The Stoop for Robbie Paul, who had guested there for Harlequins at union during the winter. He briefed his Bulls on what to expect at the tight little ground that lies in the shadows of the infamous RFU headquarters at Twickenham.

"The Stoop has a good pitch. The grass is long, but the ground is well looked after. You can get a great atmosphere in there with a good sized crowd. We're sure there'll be thousands travelling down from Bradford and that will hype us up."

Robbie also knew what to expect from the Broncos.

"I think the Broncos will be the dark-horses for every competition this season. From what we've heard they've had great preparation at their training camp in Australia. The game we played last season at The Valley was, for me, the hardest we had all year. It was such a physical game. They weren't the most exciting team, but they got through their plays well and had a very low error count

"It's going to be a very tough game. Both teams have Australian coaches with different methods, and there will be a few personal duels between our Aussies and their Aussies. It's like a local derby for some of the guys. I don't know why, but some of these Aussies hate each other! Us Kiwis are all mates though," he laughed.

"It's going to be a battle. These are the games that prove if you're up to the job. Last year we had an easy ride into the semi-final, this year we're going to have to do it the hard way. But that's how it should be. Playing at Wembley is such an honour, and you have to earn your place.

"We have the playing and coaching staff to do it. And we have a lot of support behind us in the city, and that's a big advantage."

The game was to be televised on 'Grandstand', the first time the Bulls would have appeared on BBC since the spectacular 1996 final when Robbie claimed the first-ever hat-trick at Wembley. It was a fact not lost on Paul, who again illustrated his qualities as a leading ambassador for the game.

"There are still a lot of people who don't have Sky, so I hope we can put on a great show," he said. "It was a great final last year, and if we can repeat that it will create more and more interest in the game.

"We're a much stronger squad than last year, and much more complete. One of our strengths last year was that we played well as a team. If you look at Wigan they have some great individuals, like Gary Connolly and Jason Robinson. Comparing man on man they are stronger than any other team, but the thing that we did better than any other team was to play as one unit.

"I hope we can carry that through this year. We made some tremendous buys last summer, and we've strengthened further with our off-season buys. If we can play with the same team intensity as we did last year we should walk away with some silverware this time."

The Bulls went one step closer to Robbie's prediction with a hard-earned 34-12 win at The Stoop against a formidable London Broncos side. Bradford were leaner, meaner and more clinical as they carved up the Broncos defence, running in six tries in heavy conditions.

"I think most of the press mentioned before the game that we would miss Martin Offiah. They were probably justified," said Broncos' owner Barry Maranta, as the Bulls continually spun the ball wide and found acres of space. They blitzed the Broncos right from the off, resisted a heap of pressure for the next half-hour and then simply turned on the style.

Steve McNamara was inspirational throughout and set up the first try for Paul Loughlin, playing on the wing and a half a stone heavier than last season, after just two minutes.

London drove upfield manfully but were unable to penetrate the Bulls' line and as the game wore on, the match slipped inexorably from London's clutches.

Loughlin had an almost identical replay of his try disallowed by referee David Campbell for a forward pass, minutes after a similar

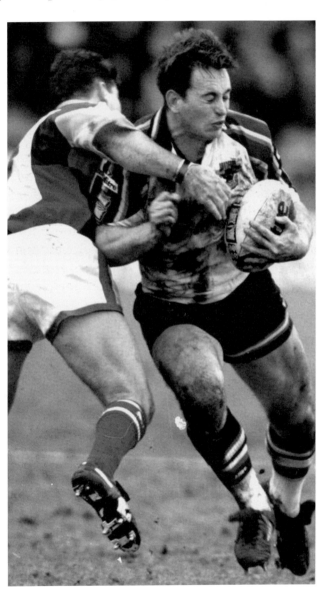

Steve McNamara guided the Bulls to a hard-earned win at London in the Challenge Cup

call on the Bulls 20. Both decisions appeared questionable and it was not lost on the 17 coachloads down from Bradford. "Cheat, cheat, cheat," they chanted, but the smiles were back on their faces minutes later when the Bulls secured an eight-point half-time cushion with a brilliant try.

Robbie Paul was the instigator, his superbly timed pass sending Bradley down the touchline supported by Sonny Nickle, who was twice involved in five clean passes, the last of which, from Lowes, saw the second row forward touchdown.

New Broncos director Richard Branson appeared at half-time to give an enthusiastic television interview on the game. "Hopefully, we'll be as big as football one day," said the multi-millionaire tycoon. "It was a fun first-half," he added.

The last 40 minutes were certainly no fun for London. A lightening break from Paul up the left touchline seemed certain to create a try for the supporting Peacock inside him, but Broncos centre David Krause managed to get between them.

James Lowes then reinforced the Bulls' authority, taking control up the middle of the field. He burst one tackle, side-stepped, drew the defence towards the left, and slipped the ball to Nickle who sprinted 30 yards to cross the line for his second try of the match. At 16-2, the huge travelling Bulls support engaged party mode.

Their heroes turned on the power that matched, and indeed bettered, anything they produced the previous season, and a hallmark try from Paul ended any hopes the Broncos had of turning the game around. As they tired, their defence slackened, and the Bulls ran in two more converted tries from Glen Tomlinson and Paul Cook, the latter with fresh legs sprinting 60 yards on the final play of the game

Elliott was quietly pleased with the performance against "tough opponents".

"It was our first real test on the back end of four months of preparation. There are more variables at the moment and after five or six matches you get to iron out some little anomalies. We executed poorly on three or four try-scoring opportunities, and we surrendered possession needlessly, but we are a side that is going to make errors because of the style of football we play. We need to accept that. The exciting thing for me is that we can get so much better."

London captain Terry Matterson was critical of his side's performance.

"I thought they were hungrier than us and faster around the paddock throughout," he admitted.

"I thought our defence was very sub-standard, very loose, especially up the middle. It probably comes down to them wanting to win more on the day. Our execution wasn't very good.

"We have to look towards the beginning of the Super League season on March 16 and build towards that."

While the Broncos licked their wounds and prepared for Super League, the Bulls were handed an away tie for the third successive game. This time it was a little nearer home, across the Pennines at Oldham, and again the Bulls romped to an ultimately convincing 38-12 win.

But despite the scoreline, it was a very competitive game. The Bulls' preparation had been disrupted when Paul Loughlin and Bernard Dwyer, making their own way to Boundary Park from their St Helens homes, arrived late thanks to a traffic snarl-up.

"Driving with Bernard is a white-knuckle ride at the best of times,"

Graeme Bradley takes on Oldham's Howard Hill
in the Challenge Cup tie at Boundary Park

Loughlin laughed. "That's why I'm going grey. We broke the land-speed record. We thought Matthew would have left us out of the team."

The former GB centre hadn't lose his sense of humour.

"When we got out of the car we found we were on the wrong side of the ground, so we had to run all the way round to get to the changing rooms," he explained. "So at least we had done our warm up."

The unorthodox preparation didn't seem to do Loughlin any harm - he powered through Oldham winger Scott Ranson for the first try after just four minutes to continue his rich seam of form in his new position on the wing.

"I've got four from three games, which is my best start ever," he revealed after the game.

"In the past it's always been me putting the winger away. It's a bit of a surprise to be playing on the wing. You expect to move inside to the pack when you're getting on a bit. I would rather play centre but I don't really mind and the coach hasn't just stuck me on the wing. He's told me to roam about, he wants me and Danny Peacock to keep switching over, and from scrums he's told me to get the ball away."

Loughlin formed a heavy-weight wing pairing with Jon Scales, and both players often packed down at loose forward.

"It's the first time I've really got stuck into the weights," Loughlin continued. "All the lads, even the smaller blokes, are lifting big weights with the work Carl Jennings has done with us, but I usually train with Graeme Bradley, Jon Scales and Matt Calland - we're basically the same build. Hopefully it will pay off for me by adding a few more years to my career - I'm 30 in July."

The Bulls' extra strength was evident against Oldham, and the Bears line cracked again soon after Loughlin's try when Lowes made a half-break and fullback Stuart Spruce was on hand to take to score from close-range.

Oldham thought they had pulled themselves back into it when Ranson lofted a harmless-looking kick and chased it. The Bulls hesitated and the Oldham winger dived on the ball as it crossed the line. But which line? One of the disadvantages of playing Rugby League on a soccer pitch is that there are so many of them! The in-goal judge disallowed the "try", but the incident seemed to inspire the home side and they pulled it back to 6-12.

But the Bulls soaked up the pressure and waited patiently for an opportunity to strike. When that opportunity came, it was executed with clinical precision.

The ball went to ground during a rare Oldham excursion into Bulls territory, Bradley snapped up the loose ball, made 40 metres and linked to set Peacock free, and the Aussie demonstrated blistering pace to score in the opposite corner of the ground.

A spell of three tries in eleven minutes early in the second half sealed the semi-final place. Robbie Paul flew outside David Bradbury to score his usual solo effort before substitute Sonny Nickle, who arrived at the ground after kick-off having been stuck in the same traffic jam as Loughlin and Dwyer, powered into a three-man tackle close to the Oldham posts and slipped the ball out for the eager Glen Tomlinson to score.

And then Paul displayed his class again when a huge Bradley kick eluded the Oldham fullback. As the ball bounced high, Paul flipped it in mid-air to his on-rushing halfback partner Tomlinson who scorched 30 metres for his second try.

"I thought we were lucky early," admitted Elliott. "We scored some lucky tries and that put Oldham off their game a little bit. I thought we were down physically today, but I am very happy with the result. It was pretty resounding, and I was a lot happier with the second half.

"It's a bit like having a child that gets 60 out of 100 in a test when you know they are capable of getting 90 out of 100. I am pleased they passed but I will look for the other 30 marks on Friday night, otherwise we'll be in some strife.

"There was a little bit of anxiety in the dressing sheds before the match with our people coming from Lancashire. I don't think it's an excuse but it is a bit of a distraction. It made me personally very anxious. It's a 17-man game so it's nice to have them all there on time, but saying that we couldn't have started the game much better. Maybe I'll tell the guys to arrive late every week."

The following day, eager Bulls fans and players switched on their televisions for the semi-final draw. There was probably no need to go through the motions. Everyone was already predicting the Bulls would be paired with Leeds, and sure enough, when the balls were drawn, the local rivals were once again pitted against each other.

It meant a repeat of the 1996 semi-final, and the venue would be the same too. Huddersfield's McAlpine Stadium is forever implanted in the hearts of Bulls fans as the place where Bullmania really took off following that sensational victory. Another chance to embarrass the Rhinos had them snapping up tickets at a fast rate of knots, but Elliott was determined to steer his players minds to the start of Super League, now less than five days away.

3
THE QUEST BEGINS

SITTING quietly in a corner of the dressing room with a cold tin of beer, Elliott reflected on a special night. A very special night.

The Bulls had just opened the second season of Super League in scintillating fashion. Elliott's team had rattled up 58 points against Warrington Wolves amid a cacophony of noise and an electric atmosphere which had seemed a totally unrealisable dream just a few years ago at Odsal. The club which had set the all-embracing entertainment package the previous season had promised that it would become even bigger and better, both on and off the pitch. No-one was disappointed.

Fireworks, pulsating music, live singers and well-drilled dancing girls supplied the pre-match party atmosphere that continued with an awesome display of power play on the field that totally overwhelmed the shell-shocked Wolves.

Even a hat-trick from skipper Robbie Paul and 22 points from playmaker Steve McNamara, was not enough to guarantee the man of the match award, as the Bulls' powerhouse pack steam-rolled over a hapless Wolves defence.

The Bulls wasted no time in delighting the vast majority of a bumper 15,017 opening night crowd when Paul finished off an incisive drive down the middle by James Lowes and early substitute Tahi Reihana.

Three minutes later Graeme Bradley, who declared himself fit only that morning after a second opinion on his broken thumb, released winger Jon Scales, whose 17 stone frame accelerated unstoppably around Mateaki Mafi to score again.

In-form goal-machine McNamara converted both tries on his way to a nine out of eleven tally as an expectant buzz rang around the vast arena.

Bradford's good approach work occasionally fell down in the last quarter, but it was little surprise when Paul skipped around four tackles

Packed terraces at Odsal for the opening night of Super League II

to re-assert their authority.

The Wolves still had some dangerous moments, however, and they created an overlap with smart passing for Chris Rudd to go in at the corner.

But any glimmer of hope Wolves harboured at half-time was quickly quashed when the Bulls ran in four tries in the first 15 minutes of the second half.

Full-back Stuart Spruce, popping up all over the field, sliced through several tackles to score, then a McNamara long pass to Paul Loughlin set Paul up for his hat-trick. Sheer strength took hard charging prop Brian McDermott over, before McNamara found himself free on the left, with two men still outside him who were not needed.

At 42-8, with less than an hour gone, the floodgates creaked and strained.

But a penalty try, awarded after a television replay, when Tony Tatupu was held on his back and had the ball wrenched from his grasp, unexpectedly sparked a mini revival. Minutes later Nigel Vagana released Andy Currier to touch down, with Jon Roper goaling both to salvage respectability for the Cheshire side.

It was only a blip in the Bulls' relentless charge to victory, as another Spruce try, a fine and richly deserved effort from James Lowes, and a last minute touchdown by Danny Peacock capped the performance.

Robbie Paul was quick to acknowledge the part the crowd played in

Brian McDermott stretches out to score against
Warrington as the Bulls get off to a flyer.

getting the Bulls' Super League campaign off to such a magnificent start.

"We won every home game last year until our final match against Halifax when we were narrowly beaten," he remembered.

"That was a shame, but this year we intend to go unbeaten at Odsal. We want to make it a place where everybody dreads coming to play.

"We are very proud of our home stadium and our support. The boys work very hard out in the community during the week, and it means a lot to us when they repay us by turning up in their thousands like they did tonight .

"Their effect is unmeasurable - you just cannot imagine how much pride and passion can be pulled off those terraces.

"We can build on that by winning. We did a lot of things well last year, but as everyone keeps saying, we didn't win any silverware. We want this year to be the year of the Bulls. It might not come about, but we are going to die trying.

"We can double tonight's performance. We're still rusty. In my case I'm still trying to feel the team movement. The rest have been training together since November, whereas I've only had three games to get prepared since coming back from rugby union."

"I was a little disappointed with my involvement, but I will work on it and hopefully it will improve."

Wolves coach John Dorahy was almost speechless.

"It was a bitterly disappointing performance."

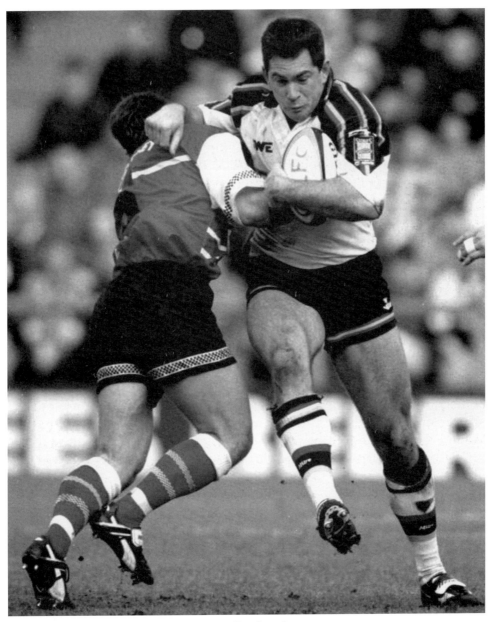

Jeremy Donougher started the season in outstanding form, but a
broken ankle at Oldham forced him out for much of the season.

"We made too many basic errors and defended poorly. We have a lot
of work still to do."

On Iestyn Harris, and his late withdrawal through injury, Dorahy was
outspoken.

"If Harris wasn't good enough to go on then I am a monkey's uncle,"
he said. "I am certainly not happy with him. Once the decision is made
for him to go then good riddance.

"He said he had a crocked thigh, but it didn't stop him apparently playing football with some lads for 90 minutes on Wednesday."

Controversy surrounded the Bulls next success, a 30-18 win at Boundary Park, the new home of Oldham Bears.

The Bears were trailing 24-18 when, in the 75th minute of a compelling, raw-boned struggle, their skipper Martin Crompton was held up over the line by Stuart Spruce.

The Bears had no argument with referee Russell Smith's ruling that Spruce prevented Crompton from grounding the ball. But after the game Spruce admitted to tackling Crompton by his skull-cap. Oldham believe that was illegal, and should have been awarded a penalty try.

"At first I thought it was just one of those tackles in a million - he did really well," said the Oldham skipper. "But he definitely got me by my skull-cap to stop me scoring, so it should have been a penalty try.

"It's disappointing when things like that go against you, because that's what these referees are well paid for. Something so blatant should be picked up. If he had given the penalty try it would have been 24-all, and I would have fancied us to win."

But RFL referees chief Greg McCallum explained that tackles by the scrum cap are not necessarily illegal.

"There is a rule that says that if a tackler removes a player's scrum cap he should be penalised," said McCallum. "But as far as tackling by the scrum cap, there is no law that says you can't, although any tackle around the head would be brought into question. Pulling someone by the scrum cap is the same as pulling someone by the head, which is not against the rules."

Despite that, defeat was cruel on Oldham. They battled heroically against a stuttering Bulls outfit, and led 14-12 at half-time.

But the Bulls were always the more dangerous side, and looked set for a repeat of their comfortable Challenge Cup win when Steve McNamara and Warren Jowitt powered through for tries in the opening minutes.

And when Graeme Bradley shrugged off Scott Ranson to regain an 18-14 lead three minutes into the second half the Bulls looked ready to run away with the game.

But Oldham didn't capitulate. Jeremy Donougher was forced to make a brilliant try-saving tackle on Crompton, one of a number of crucial contributions by the Aussie back-rower until he suffered the cruel break of an ankle midway through the half that was to rule him out for much of the season.

Robbie Paul, an increasing threat throughout the match, stepped up a gear and began to steer the Bulls to safety.

Ranson denied him once with a superb cover tackle, but the Oldham

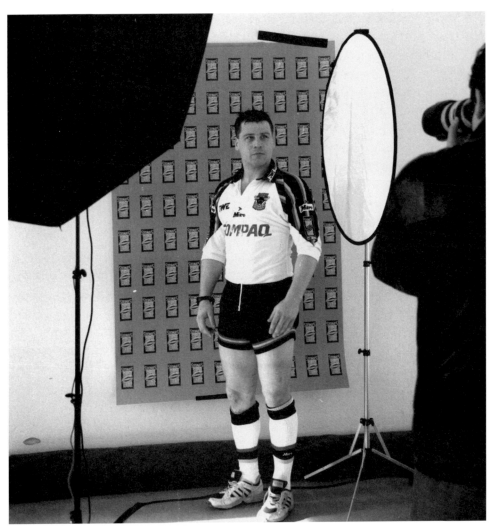

James Lowes poses for the mandatory publicity
photographs during the first week of the season.

winger was at fault minutes later when he dived over Glen Tomlinson's
kick for Spruce to score a try which, with McNamara's conversion,
created a ten-point lead.

Oldham cut the gap to six points and then came Spruce's 'tackle in a
million' - legal or not.

On the last play of the game Sonny Nickle powered over from close
range to complete a 12-point margin which even the Bulls conceded was
flattering.

Rather than criticise his players, however, coach Matthew Elliott
preferred to praise Oldham and count his blessings .

"I reminded the guys that we lost a similar match early last season to
Sheffield. I told them to remember this one - it could make a difference

down the track. While tactically and technically we were not at our best, it was nice to see that we could dig in for the win.

"Oldham certainly weren't the same side I saw at Leeds last week. They gave us a lesson in enthusiasm and commitment."

But the game provided one of those special moments that helps bond player and coach.

At half-time, a furious Elliott hadn't held back in delivering a blistering verdict on the first forty minutes. He stormed up and down the Boundary Park dressing room, banging his fists on the treatment table, scattering anything that was unfortunate enough to be in his way.

"I was really fed up," Elliott recalled. "We were in front but we were very poor. There's a certain drama involved with coaching, and I'd delivered a strong and forceful message to them. I wasn't ranting and raving but I'd made my point very clear. I turned away, went out of the door and pulled it with all my strength to make it slam very loudly. Trouble was, the damn thing was one of those with a hydraulic closing mechanism. Very slowly and quietly it eased itself shut with a gentle click. I stood there shaking my head and thought, what have I done.

"I went back in because that gave me the double wobblies. I poked my head gingerly through the door and saw seventeen smiling faces peering back at me. For a few seconds there was silence and then we all had a good giggle. It did the trick though!"

It wouldn't be the last time Elliott and his team shared a joke.

"I probably lost my sense of humour as the season went on because the pressure increased as the stakes were raised. But on most occasions, even when we go through the most horrific video session and I have to point a sharp finger at a player in front of his mates, we still manage to have a laugh. It's important that we remember we have to be serious in what we do but it's just as important to inject a little humour. The players know I have a weakness in that I wet myself laughing at them. They're a great group, and if we lost our sense of humour Bradford Bulls as a team would be worse for it."

4
BACK AT WEMBLEY

STANDING in the path of a second successive Wembley appearance was, as the year before, arch-rivals Leeds Rhinos.

The disappointment of losing out the previous year was still hurting the Rhinos. They had been hot favourites to win through to their third consecutive final in 1996, but the up-coming Bulls weren't working off the same script and shocked everyone in storming to a 28-6 win.

Twelve months on, the tables had been turned. Now it was the Rhinos who were underdogs, and the pressure was firmly on the Bulls thanks to unprecedented media interest in the club and the ever-increasing hordes of supporters desperate to see their heroes hoist some silverware.

One Bull was keener than most to satisfy those hungry fans. Jon Scales had been shown the door at Headingley during the Centenary Season, but the blockbusting winger had proved to be the bargain buy in the Bulls' rebuilding programme.

With a regular first team spot, and a contract to take him up to the new century, the £25,000 acquisition had become a vital member of the huge Bulls' backline. He had scored a memorable hat-trick in that 1996 semi-final, a game that signalled the emergence of the Bulls - and Scales - as major players, and twelve months on he was keen to repeat the punishment on his old club.

"It's always nice to play against your old club and come out on top. But it's a totally different Leeds side now to the one I left. I see Gary Mercer occasionally, but he's the only one .

"It's hard to assess just how good Leeds are. We were the underdogs last year but this time it's Leeds who haven't anything to lose. They are an unknown quantity this season. They've brought in several new players, including some Australians, that nobody knows too much about. But if we play as well as we can I think we'll go through."

Warren Jowitt began to realise his enormous potential in the early part of the season.

Scales was aware of the huge expectation now surrounding the Bulls.

"We came from nowhere to finish third in the league last summer. The pressure is on us now, because everyone expects us to do well. We've built ourselves up to be the best supported team in Super League, and the crowd for our opening game against Warrington showed how much further interest the club has generated during the off-season.

"A lot of new fans have been attracted to Odsal, and they expect us to win something. We were unlucky in last year's final, but now we must move forward and prove that we are good enough to win some silverware."

In the build-up to the semi-final, many sections of the media were still questioning the Bulls' ability to improve on the previous campaign. Even the blistering start to the league, with six straight wins going into the semi, wasn't enough to convince everyone. Some even suggested the Bulls were still relying on the hangover of Brian Smith's influence. Scales dismissed suggestions that the Bulls would suffer from the premature loss of Smith.

"Matthew did most of the coaching last season anyway. Brian was more of a chief executive. He had a massive influence, but Matthew did most of the work out on the training field.

"Things have carried on in the same vein, with Matthew just tweaking things a little. He will be a successful coach in his own right."

Scales, like the other Bulls players, took nothing for granted.

"We had a good workout at Oldham. It was a difficult game, because we had beaten them convincingly just two weeks earlier. Perhaps we thought we'd do the same again, but they shocked us early on and had us on the back foot. That's probably what we needed a week before the semi-final, because it got rid of any complacency that might have been there."

Scales watched St Helens demolish Salford in the other semi-final the week before, but firmly believed that the Bulls' name was on the Challenge Cup this year.

"I thought Salford had some bad luck early on. To beat Saints they had to be at their very best, and they needed the rub of the green with the referee's decisions.

"We are a much stronger team than last year, and if we can get past Leeds I think we'll win it this time.

"We all want to get to Wembley again, but the priority for us is Super League and the World Club Championship. I think we'll go well this year."

Scales couldn't repeat his hat-trick heroics of the year before, but the Bulls achieved the same end result. The 24-10 win was, to be honest, quite flattering. It was a real bruiser of a game and became one of the most controversial eighty minutes of the year. It had more spite than spice, and was mean, hard and at times fiercely illegal.

But it was also rivetting viewing. If you looked away for a second you missed something, whether it was a punch or a breathtaking attack.

Leeds were determined not to be easy-beats again and were fired up for a do-or-die battle. From the moment the teams emerged from the plush McAlpine Stadium dressing rooms and charged towards each other for the first bone-crunching tackle, the impact was explosive.

Steve McNamara crashes over for the gamebreaking try minutes after half-time in the semi-final against Leeds.

Tempers flare as James Lowes and Gary Mercer square up to each other after Lowes had scored the Bulls opening try.

Leeds went ahead after only six minutes, when Phil Hassan took advantage of a favourable bounce from Graham Holroyd's high kick to send Tony Kemp flashing in at the corner.

They constantly had the Bulls under intense pressure, and nearly thirty minutes had gone before the Bulls wound up the power to dig out a James Lowes try, goaled by Steve McNamara. It was a vital break-through and emphasised the increasing importance of Lowes to the Bulls. The hooker exploited Leeds' over-eager defence near their own line to chip through and win the scramble for the touchdown. Throughout the game he caused his old club problems with short, stabbing runs that ripped into the belly of Leeds' defence. Add a top tackle count of 30, and it was almost enough for the official Silk Cut man of the match award just ahead of actual winner Paul Medley.

But Medley was a deserved winner, making an enormous impact in his two substitute appearances, totalling just under an hour of full-blooded commitment. It revived bitter-sweet memories for Headingley fans of his late substitute role for Leeds in ripping Bradford apart and earning the man of the match award in a Yorkshire Cup tie nine years before. Then, as now, he pounded over 40 metres for a great solo try. But it did not stop Malcolm Reilly selling him to Halifax soon after, adding to the belief that the Leeds coach thought he "lacked bottle".

That was always an unfair charge. He had since developed into a 100% committed forward who never took a step backwards. Against Leeds, he couldn't wait to get into the heat of battle and, when he did, the Leeds pack had to gang up to stop him - and didn't always succeed.

Medley epitomises the modern 17-man interchange game, which hopefully reached a peak in the semi-final, having 14 substitutions and blood-bin exchanges. Add three dismissals to the sinbin, plus a permanent sending off, and it was almost impossible to keep track of all the comings and goings.

For a brief time it was twelve Bulls against eleven Rhinos, and it proved a crucial period, as Bradford scored two tries and went 16-14 ahead. Sonny Nickle and Rhino Phil Hassan had gone to cool off after trading blows in the 33rd minute, and Leeds centre Richie Blackmore soon joined them for interfering at a play-the-ball with Bradford poised to strike near the line.

Paul Loughlin took advantage of the gap in the Leeds centre to dummy through just before the interval and, within three minutes of the restart, McNamara did the same as the first two sinners were returning.

McNamara added the goal, and a penalty a few minutes later, to put Bradford 18-4 clear.

But there was still plenty of fight in Leeds - interpret that any way you like - and they tore back at the Bulls, with Martin Masella highlighting a powerful game up front with a rampaging run that took him over the line to bring Leeds closer at 18-10.

Then Medley came back on to finish off Leeds with his magnificent try, following good approach play by Robbie Paul and Loughlin.

"It's nice to get a try at any time, never mind in a semi-final, but all credit to the lads who put me away," said a delighted Medley afterwards. "Once I saw the try line I just wanted to get there. I knew that I would get on the field at some stage, because Matthew is always saying that it's a seventeen-man game, but even I was surprised when it was so early in the game. It was a great game to play in."

Medley's try should have sent away everyone except the Leeds fans with a final, glowing memory of the game. But it was obscured by a brutal last round as the Bulls' Brian McDermott resumed his professional boxing days with a perfect right cross to Terry Newton that led to his 75th minute dismissal.

Matthew Elliott later claimed that several of his players had a variety of facial wounds, and slammed referee Russell Smith for not protecting his players.

"As delighted as I am with the win, I was upset with the way the game went, and felt that the players were in very great danger out on the field," fumed Elliott.

The victorious Bulls celebrate their semi-final win

"There were a lot of fat lips, head knocks, slight concussions and stitches in the mouths of my players back in the dressing room, and I have to say that is all down to a man who failed to stamp his authority on the game.

"My complaints have nothing to do with Leeds or the way they played. Rugby League is a very physical game and, as in all walks of life, players will try to get away with what they are allowed to get away with.

"In the end it was us who ended up having a player sent off, which I felt was ludicrous in the light of some of the things that had gone on before."

The RFL's Referees' Coaching Director Greg McCallum moved quickly to diffuse the situation.

"There are a number of issues that concern me regarding tackling and verballing by players from both sides," he said, after spending most of the following day viewing the video tape of the game.

"There were also two incidents in the last few minutes where the touch judge correctly ruled against two Leeds tries, but appears to be quite aggressively verballed by the players. The League only has one rule regarding that, and we'll make sure it doesn't happen again."

McCallum also fired a broadside at the Bulls coach.

"The bye-laws of the game state there is to be no public criticism of referees. We'll look at his comments and decide whether he went outside the rules.

"I thought Russell Smith got a lot of the big calls right and he was well supported by his touch judges. His performance will be judged by what happens this week about the tackles. We have the benefit of video tapes and all decisions will be made without emotion."

But McCallum revealed that Smith was still in the reckoning for the Final.

"Russell hasn't done himself any great harm. David Campbell is going well, and the guys who are impressing us are Steve Presley and Bob Connolly."

McCallum's comments did little to pacify the angry Elliott.

"I am just delighted to be back at Wembley after a very tough game. I knew it would be a different proposition to last year and that Leeds are a vastly different outfit who were always going to be formidable opponents.

"But I really felt that players were in great danger out there. I know back in Australia that you can be fined $10,000 for having a go at the officials, but I feel criticism is justified this time and my complaints have nothing to do with Leeds or the way they played.

"If there was national disaster and looters go unchecked, then there are more looters back the next day. You have to enforce the law to stop the law being violated. There was a professional put in the middle of the park and I am afraid he just didn't do his job. I was not happy with his performance in our game at Oldham and I was not happy this time. I need to talk to Greg McCallum to sort this out as I feel I have a responsibility to my players to get the matter resolved.

"In the end it was us who ended up having a player sent off. I feel that Brian McDermott finally let his frustrations get the better of him and vented his feelings. I was disappointed that he reacted in such a manner that he got himself sent off. But it astounds me that such a ruling could be made after what had happened before. It was a physical game but the fact that no one was seriously injured was through good luck and not the efforts of the match official.

"The instances that went unchecked and unpunished were such that someone could seriously have been hurt. The man who could have helped to avert any such injuries did not assert his influence until there were just four minutes left, and by then the frustration was just oozing out."

But Elliott acknowledged the much-improved Rhinos performance.

"Leeds played well and put us under a lot of early pressure that brought them a try from a cruel bounce of the ball. But even though we suffered that setback I never felt that we were in any danger of losing the game. I always felt confident even though we lost continuity at times.

"I thought Paul Medley made a big impact even though he was forced into the game early, and that Brian McDermott and James Lowes could have pushed him close for the man of the match award. I also thought that Stuart Spruce really brought us alive in the second half with three try-saving tackles. He was brilliant, and when you have someone like him at the back then it gives the rest of the team confidence to get on with their jobs. Leeds tested us with some high quality kicks but Stuart was up to the test each time.

"I know that my starting line-up surprised a few people but I picked who I thought was best to handle a Leeds team as I thought it would be. They surprised me by leaving Barrie McDermott on the bench, but that was the only surprise. We focussed inwardly on their potential danger men and key plays all week and I decided it would be best to have Graeme Bradley at stand-off, move Paul Loughlin to the centre and bring Paul Cook on to the wing, with Glen Tomlinson onto the bench. I know that players don't like starting on the bench, but I have to drum it into them that this is now a seventeen-man game and that all my substitutes will play a significant part in the game at some stage.

A jubilant Paul Medley leaves the McAlpine pitch after coming off the bench twice to have an enormous impact.

"That is what they all did, with Glen coming on for Steve McNamara when I thought he looked like he was starting to tire. And no wonder. He had got through a terrific amount of work. The game was intensely contested with just a small number of key points, and when you look at those, Paul Loughlin's try just before half-time came at just the right moment to send us in on a high.

"But if I look for the factor that gave us the win rather than Leeds I would have to say that it was our all-round effort that was our major contributor. Leeds did well in an outstanding game, but we worked that little bit harder and got our reward."

Despite his frustrations, Elliott found it hard to conceal his joy at taking the Bulls back to Wembley so soon in his fledgling coaching career.

"I am really looking forward to going back again, and this time I will be leading the side out. Last year I was the assistant but this time it is my team, and I am going to enjoy it. Brian (Smith) and myself speak on a weekly basis, and I know he will be delighted that we have reached the Final again.

"We are a better team that we were twelve months ago, but we are still learning and have plenty of room for improvement. We will be ready to take on St Helens."

Skipper Robbie Paul echoed his coach.

"Last year I don't remember the game, but I just have a whole collection of emotions to recall. Its good to be back and we're all looking forward to it.

"Against Leeds it was a physical battle, and we all have bumps and bruises to show for it, but we are a more complete side, and that is what won the day for us.

"It was a difficult game for us to win, but we approached it with a positive attitude and came through."

Fullback Stuart Spruce shed tears of joy as he walked into the dressing room. Twelve months earlier, as a Widnes player, he had suffered the heartbreak of losing a semi-final.

"I have to admit that this is a much better feeling," he smiled. "I thought we did well to win through, especially after that terrible bounce left Cookie stranded and allowed Kemp to score early on.

"But we came back in a physical game, and then held on when they put the pressure on in the final stages. I thought we had the game won by then, but I was delighted to be able to turn Francis Cummins on his back, and then to tackle Rivett. They were important tries to stop, because who knows what would have happened if either of those chances had been taken. They could have given them the heart to get another score."

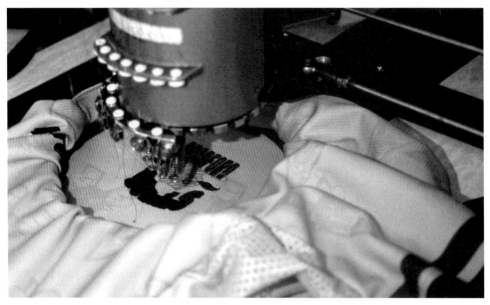

The Bulls were forced into producing a new shirt for Wembley when St Helens refused to change to their away strip.

Spruce then turned towards his team-mates, let out a yell of satisfaction and joined in the celebrations as press photographers clamoured for the pictures that would adorn the following morning's papers.

Whilst the scenes of undiluted jubilation continued in the dressing room, and on the Bradford road out of Huddersfield that was jammed solid with a convoy of Bulls supporters blowing their car horns and dangling scarves out of the windows, less enjoyable scenes were unfolding upstairs in the McAlpine's banqueting suite.

RFL officials were attempting to extinguish a simmering row between St Helens and the Bulls over who would wear which kit for the showpiece final. Saints had won the first semi-final two weeks earlier and had assumed they would automatically wear their first choice kit. But when it was pointed out that both the Bulls home and away kits would clash, Saints were asked to switch to their blue and yellow alternative. They steadfastly refused, and the only solution was a toss of a coin. The Bulls lost and Saints continued to insist on wearing their home colours of red, white and black.

"We want the opportunity to give our playing strip the widest possible exposure," said Saints' chief executive David Howes. "The bye-laws state that there can't be a colour clash, so Bradford will have to commission a new kit. It's a tight schedule, but it is possible."

The Bulls argued, quite rightly, that the easiest option was for Saints to wear blue. After all, that kit was already manufactured and on general sale as recognised St Helens merchandise. The RFL were asked to insist Saints made the change to blue, but they decided it wasn't within their power to make that ruling and the reluctant Bulls were left with only one option. They would have to design, commission and manufacture a complete new strip for just one game. Already faced with the massive workload that a Wembley final brings, Peter Deakin suddenly had another major headache to contend with.

"We spoke to Mitre as soon as we realised Saints wouldn't budge. My main concern was not in putting the new kit together, but in how the fans would react. We had achieved record sales of replica shirts leading up to the semi-final, and now they were being told the Bulls wouldn't be wearing either of the two recognised kits at Wembley. There was a real danger that we could alienate them and be tarred with the same brush as soccer clubs, who seem to have a blatant disregard for fans by changing their kit every season.

"So we decided not to offer the new kit for sale. We announced through the press that we were making a one-off limited edition kit to celebrate the Centenary of the Challenge Cup. We got to work on designing the new kit and, though we didn't admit it at the time, to be honest it wasn't that big a problem. We had already begun work on a new shirt for the World Club Championship games that would only be worn for that series and offered for sale as replicas with special badging. The design for that shirt was already agreed, so all we did for Wembley was use the same patterns and changed the colour from white to amber."

The new kit was hurriedly assembled at Mitre's factory in Bolton. Deakin made several visits to check on progress and cast a keen eye over detail. Eventually he was happy, and the new shirt was unveiled in *Super League Week* magazine just days before the final.

Deakin manipulated his close relationship with the press and the shirt won instant approval from the fans. A potentially awkward situation had been turned into a major publicity coup. In the build-up to the final they received much more exposure because of their new kit than they would have normally expected as photographers and TV crews anxiously snatched pictures of the much talked about new colours.

St Helens stubbornness had turned out to be a huge bonus.

5

GATHERING MOMENTUM

CELEBRATIONS at once again reaching Wembley were shortlived. Just three days after the McAlpine triumph the Bulls got back to the bread and butter of league action with a Tuesday night trip to Castleford.

Historically, Wheldon Road is one of the less fruitful hunting grounds, and despite their unbeaten start to the season the Bulls were worried that the euphoria of the semi-final win might carry over. They needn't have worried. The Bulls had little trouble gaining a 38-12 victory that took them back to the top of the table and sent Castleford to the bottom.

Compared to the fiery game against Leeds it was a tame affair, and Matthew Elliott had no doubts why.

"This was a pretty good advertisement of why it's best not to play two games in one week. I thought both sides lacked some oomph.

"Collectively, I thought my players were really good tonight, but they didn't run quite as well as they can, or tackle as hard as they can. You can't blame the players for that. As the game gets quicker and the players get more powerful, stronger and fitter it takes longer to recover.

"Our fans were fantastic again and I would liked to have given them the type of spectacular performance we are capable of."

The Bulls went to Castleford missing several of the players who starred in the semi-final win. Gary Christie got his first start in twelve months on the wing, prop Paul Anderson was on debut after his move from Halifax, and Nathan Graham and Simon Knox made it onto the bench.

The hectic start to the season was proving costly. Warren Jowitt was stretchered off with a broken ankle mid-way through the second half to join Jeremy Donougher on the sidelines as a long term absentee. It was a particularly bad blow for Jowitt, who was making the most of only his second start with the Bulls after a succession of impressive substitute appearances. The young second-rower had powered in for a 37th minute try and suffered his injury after another typical full-blooded run of 40 metres.

Jowitt's try came off a pass from Robbie Paul, one of many delightful touches he showed in a dazzling performance crowned by a special piece of magic minutes from the end, when he ghosted through near halfway, flitted inside one tackle and then another before moving away to the posts. It was one of Paul's best-ever games in a Bulls shirt. He opened the try-scoring in the fifth minute, following smart play by his half-back partner Glen Tomlinson, and continued to provide most of the entertainment in an otherwise lack lustre match.

Castleford rarely threatened and showed only fleeting glimpses of enterprise in a game dominated by the Bulls, whose other tries highlighted their all round competence. Paul Loughlin slipped easily through off Steve McNamara's pass, Tomlinson sent Brian McDermott charging under the posts and James Lowes kicked ahead twice for his touchdown.

All cause for quiet satisfaction for Bradford coach Elliott, who was far happier with the match officials than he had been three days earlier.

"I thought they were all outstanding," he said. "The referee who has a good rapport with the players finds it a lot easier to control the game and tonight's referee had a great rapport."

On the Sunday, the Bulls returned to Odsal for the game of the round and the stiffest challenge yet to their unbeaten start.

Second-placed London Broncos were the visitors and a huge 15,000-plus crowd, still ecstatic from the semi-final win, turned out. It was a game that even at this early stage of the season would give a real pointer to the championship ambitions of both teams.

"All the games are hard now," agreed Sonny Nickle before the game. "We've had a few tough games recently and have managed to come through unbeaten but now we have to turn it on again against London.

"They have a lot of new players and they'll get stronger as the season goes on. I think now they've had a few games together they're looking a good side and are performing well. They'll be much tougher than they were when we played them in the Challenge Cup, but we've got home advantage and at Odsal, with the big crowds, that counts for a lot."

Nickle's thoughts were already set firmly on winning the Super League crown.

"The game today is so hard and intense. We want to win Super League and that means winning week in, week out. Saints are the obvious choice and London will be there or thereabouts. Everybody is waiting to see who drops points first because once a side falls just two or four points behind it's a hell of a gap to make up. Last season Saints lost just two games, and that's how it will be again this year. Those clubs who have already lost two or three can forget the championship. There's no let up and you can't let your concentration lapse. Wigan perhaps did that at Warrington the other week and look what happened to them."

Ahead of the Broncos game, Elliott had a few selection worries. Jowitt was in plaster up to his knee after his break at Castleford, and Steve McNamara had pulled up to severely weaken Elliott's pack options.

"The upheaval of the team because of injuries has made it difficult but we have a great squad now, and those players on the fringes who have been given a chance are doing their best to stay in there," added Nickle.

"All the players are upset for Warren. He has worked very hard during the winter and was coming through well. He's a very strong runner and a valuable member of the first team squad.

"Losing Warren and Jed (Jeremy Donougher) is a big blow, and it's now that our squad depth will be tested. We have Simon Knox, Paul Anderson plus Paul Medley, who is defying his age at the moment and playing really well."

"We still haven't clicked as a team yet, but as long as we are in the right frame of mind and do what we are capable of we should win. It will be a very physical and fast game. London will be fired up and will try to knock us off our game."

Nickle wasn't wrong. The Bulls ground out a hard-earned 19-14 win, but had the match gone on another five minutes the Broncos might have snatched the points. They looked marginally the stronger of two very weary sides, both suffering from three tough games in a week. The Bulls had hard-working prop Brian McDermott on the sidelines after copping a ban for his brief bout of boxing in the semi-final, but it was the intensity of the Easter programme that was subject to criticism from both coaches as they counted their ever diminishing squads after the game.

"There were some really tired people out there. I felt sorry for our fans because we didn't play the kind of rugby we are capable of," said a relieved Elliott. "If you want high quality Rugby League we have got to look at this.

Broncos coach Tony Currie agreed, and pointed out that his squad was down to 16 players before the game, with influential second-rower Peter Gill withdrawing at the eleventh hour with a back spasm.

The Bulls got off to a dream start when Stuart Spruce picked up an awkward ball and sent the overlapping Paul Loughlin in for a try in the left hand corner. London posed plenty of problems before Steve McNamara extended the lead with a simple penalty after interference at the play the ball in front of the posts.

Broncos' second-rower Steve Rosolen was held up over the line, and then a high Matterson bomb caused some panic in the Bulls in-goal area, the ball finally being touched down by a London hand, but referee David Campbell deciding no try. Soon after, a kick from Shaun Edwards bounced wickedly for Spruce, who had no chance of beating a grateful David Krause to the ball. Greg Barwick's kick levelled the scores.

Currie cited Graeme Bradley as the reason why the Bulls managed to cling on at the end, and it was one of the Australian's charging runs which gave them back the initiative. He broke down the middle of the London defence, rounded stranded fullback Barwick and put the supporting Nickle in under the posts.

Bradley's awareness then sent Paul Cook racing in from the touchline, cutting diagonally through a mass of players to score a brilliant try. McNamara goaled both touchdowns, and the Bulls left the field with a comfortable 18-6 lead.

After the interval, two tight and well drilled defences controlled the early exchanges of the second half, easily swallowing up most offensive efforts. McNamara broke the deadlock with a timely field-goal which left London three scores in arrears. It would prove too much for the battling Broncos, but that they almost made it was a credit to Currie's beleaguered troops.

The big crowd held their breath for much of the remaining minutes but, driven on by the tireless Bradley, their heroes held on to leapfrog back over Wembley rivals St Helens to once again top the table.

The games against Castleford and London provided a breakthrough for winger Gary Christie. After twelve months in the wilderness, he had forced his way back into the frontline. The former Oldham and Wakefield winger had been a regular in the Bulls attack during the Centenary Season and played a key role in helping Bradford achieve their 1996 Wembley appearance. But suddenly his world turned upside down. He was left out of that final side, and made just two starts in the whole of Super League '96.

Such was the strength in depth that six top squad wingers were chasing the two available places. Paul Cook and Paul Loughlin were the incumbents, along with Jon Scales, Abi Ekoku, occasionally Danny Peacock, and Christie himself.

"Lockers is playing so well I think he deserves to be in the centre," said Christie with a wry smile. "He's more at home in the centre and much happier there. At least I hope he is!"

Christie started on the wing at Castleford but was back on the bench for the London game when coach Matthew Elliott decided to use Danny Peacock as a combined winger-cum-fullback. As the Bulls' crunch game

(ABOVE) Wearing the revolutionary "Body Kit", the Bulls players are put through a training session at their Rawdon Meadows headquarters.

(RIGHT) Stuart Spruce jumps for a high ball with Leeds Paul Sterling and Damian Gibson in the Challenge Cup semi-final.

(BELOW) Sonny Nickle powers through the Rhinos defence at McAlpine Stadium.

Having fun is
what the Bulls
experience is
all about.
Each game has
a theme for its
pre-match
entertainment.
Singers,
dancers,
parades of
Harley-
Davidsons,
Bullman,
jugglers,
fire-eaters
and more.
A local haulage
company even
re-painted
their trucks!

(ABOVE) Packed terracing and full hospitality boxes became the norm during the 1997 season.
(BELOW) The versatile Bernard Dwyer has been outstanding since his move from St Helens.

(ABOVE) Resplendent in their new shirts, the Bulls pose for the pre-Wembley photo-call.

(LEFT) The Bulls arrive at their St Albans base.

(BELOW) Brian McDermott is tackled during the final.

(BELOW LEFT) Stuart Spruce gets the ball away

(OPPOSITE) The Bulls players relax at Wembley the day before the final.

(FAR RIGHT) Graeme Bradley and his young son leave the Wembley pitch.

In a season plagued by injuries, Robbie Paul didn't reach the heights of his outstanding previous year, but was still the most sought-after player by fans and media.

(ABOVE) Pursuing his hobby on a rare day off; (RIGHT) playing for New Zealand; (BELOW) another television interview; (BELOW RIGHT) presenting the breakfast show on local radio with Brian McDermott.

(RIGHT) Glen Tomlinson looks to offload at London.

(BELOW) Steve McNamara's kicking game was again a major feature of the Bulls play.

(BELOW RIGHT) Coming off the bench, Nathan Graham often had a big influence.

(ABOVE) Paul Anderson quickly developed into a crowd favourite with his barnstorming runs after signing from Halifax.
(RIGHT) Danny Peacock continually broke down opposition defences.
(BELOW) Matthew Elliott watches from the bench at London.
(BELOW RIGHT) Warren Jowitt takes on the Castleford defence.

Injured Warren Jowitt and banned Brian McDermott
watch the game against London from the bench.

at Wigan loomed, Christie was again unsure whether he would keep his place.

"It's an excellent position for the club to be in," he conceded. "There is intense pressure on every place and that's why we are successful. At some clubs players know they can perhaps sit back or have a bad game and keep their place. But at Bradford one error can cost you. Look at Jon Scales. He was first choice winger last season but was dropped a couple of weeks ago and now has a hard job to get his place back."

Christie, to his credit, accepted his Wembley heartache but struggled to force his way back after several injury problems.

"It's been a hard year for me. I played in all the rounds including the semi-final but was then dropped a couple of games before the final. It's hard being a squaddie, especially for a Wembley final when you are told you are the eighteenth man. You're with the squad but at the same time are so distant. If I make the seventeen this year it will be a dream come true. I'm hopeful and I'm training harder than ever. If I don't make it I daren't think how I'd react.

"Mentally I lost it a bit. I was so disappointed to be back in the Alliance team. I'm happy at Bradford but I don't want to play in the reserves forever.

Three Bulls players had that week decided to move on for the very

Paul Cook skips past London's Greg Barwick for a try.

reason Christie highlighted. Jason Donohue and Andy Ireland went to Hull, and Tommy Hodgkinson reached a settlement on his contract but was without a club. The Lancashire based trio shared the trek along the M62 with Christie and Stuart Spruce.

"Just me and Sprogger now," sighed Christie. "It's a bit of a disappointment really but I can understand why they've left. It's demoralising when you are in the reserves every week without getting a sniff. They knew they were good enough to play first grade, although perhaps not at Bradford. Jason and Andy were man-of-the-match nearly every week but never had a chance of coming through. Hull is a long way for them to travel but it's a good move for them. Hopefully they'll be in Super League next year.

"Every player aspires to be at a top club, and I'm not about to take a step down just to get a first team place. I want to be a regular here at Bradford and now I've had a sniff again I intend to make the most of it."

While Christie was struggling to re-establish himself, Graeme Bradley was proving to be possibly the most valuable player in Super League. Known as "the Penguin" because of his awkward running style, 33 year-old Bradley had been a surprise signing by Brian Smith during his initial wave of recruitment back in the winter of 1995. Critics who had seen Bradley at Castleford in the mid-eighties questioned Bradford's wisdom in bringing the ageing centre-cum-second row back to Britain. But his acquisition proved to be a masterstroke, and he quickly became the vital cog in the Bulls machine, exerting more influence on the team than any other player and earning the respect of every other professional.

In the tense and absorbing victory over the Broncos, Bradley was the top man. He spurred his side on to overcome their weariness and mental exhaustion caused by the fixture pile-up. He began the game at the centre and ended it as virtually a prop forward, was influential in the gamebreaking tries and contributed a solid defensive stint coupled with hard, driving runs.

"It will be good to get Brian McDermott back," he grinned afterwards. "It was one of those situations where there was a fair bit of disruption to the side and we had difficulties going forward, especially second half. It was a matter of having a go. If you get your timing right you can make the yards okay. I had that role when I played second row at Castleford. I like taking the ball forward and a physical game. It suits my style - you won't see me scoring 80-metre tries like Robbie Paul. It was a case when teamwork rather than individuals won the day. We took our chances well."

Bradley highlighted one big difference with the game over here compared to Australia.

"In Britain there's a far bigger turnover of players each year than in Australia," he says. "Look at London - they're still adjusting to the amount of new players they've brought in. But by the end of the season they'll be a good side.

"We also had a few new lads like Simon Knox, Paul Anderson and Jeff Wittenberg who haven't played much first-grade with Bradford. But they have benefited from the game and it'll make us a stronger side overall."

There wasn't much time for the battered bodies and aching limbs to ease. Five days later the Bulls had to pick themselves up for a Friday night game at Wigan. If the London game had been hard, the visit to Central Park would provide the ultimate barometer of the the Bulls title ambitions.

Wigan were going through what they liked to call "a transitional period". Boardroom wrangling, a new coach, a cloud hanging over the future of their famous ground and an influx of new home-bred players had destabilised the club. The end result was a shaky start to the season by their own exacting standards, but they were still considered the team to beat and tipped by many to come good and take the Super League title.

It turned out to be one of the games of the season, a roller-coaster ride that was only decided in the final minutes when Matt Calland stepped off the bench to score the try that clinched the game and maintained the 100 per cent record.

Calland had only had his hands on the ball once when Robbie Paul and Glen Tomlinson worked it wide in the 74th minute for the substitute to crash over. It was the score that finally killed off the Warriors, who had twice come from behind to lead, only to fall to two tries in the last ten minutes. But neither coach believed it killed off Wigan's Super League chances, despite leaving them three defeats behind the Bulls and two behind the Saints, both of whom had now stormed the Central Park citadel and had gone home with the points.

"I certainly wouldn't be writing this team off," said the victorious Elliott. "They've got some new players in their outfit and they're very close to clicking. I don't think Super League will be won this year by a team only losing two games."

Warriors coach Eric Hughes agreed, while accepting that it had been a real four-pointer.

"We're not dead and buried," he claimed defiantly, "but there is daylight between us. It was a crucial game and we're bitterly disappointed to have lost. But there's a long way to go, and there will be plenty of close games. We're still capable of turning over any side in the game."

Both sides seemed to lack concentration in the early exchanges, as referee Stuart Cummings chalked up seven penalties in the first ten minutes, almost all for offences around the play the ball. Several coaches had already predicted that such offences would cost English teams dearly against their Aussie challengers in the World Club Championship.

The early flurry of penalties left the Bulls 4-2 ahead and looking the more threatening. Paul Anderson had clearly been sent out to have a big first 20 minutes before making way for Jeff Wittenberg, and Graeme Bradley was slowly taking charge of the game.

Bradley's influence grew stronger as the game went on, as coach Elliott was quick to acknowledge.

"He can play centre, second row, loose forward or anywhere. He's all over the place."

Paul Anderson on the rampage at Wigan

Former Bingley junior Simon Haughton put Wigan ahead when he charged through Sonny Nickle and Danny Peacock from 20 metres, but Peacock responded with a double, the first coming in tandem with James Lowes, who did well to offload after Peacock himself had made the decisive break.

Paul Cook's fourth successful kick edged the Bulls further ahead after the break, and when Andy Farrell failed with his next two chances the goal-kicking proved to be decisive, each side finishing with three tries.

Haughton added his second try on the hour, bravely plunging over but being injured in scoring and playing no further part. He was still trying to gather his wits when Wigan went back into the lead seven minutes later thanks to Tony Smith's first try for them since moving from Castleford. With a six-point lead, Wigan had ten minutes to hang on for a victory which would have left them just one defeat behind Bradford and St Helens.

But the Bulls would have none of it, coming back with two tries in five minutes to steal the points. Peacock scored a devastating second try when he took Paul's pass like an express train from ten metres out, although it was too far out for Cook to convert - his one failure in six attempts. The Bulls were still two points adrift, but off the bench came Calland who, after Bradley had been stopped on the line, crossed for the clincher.

With Brian McDermott and Steve McNamara absent, and Sonny Nickle lasting less than half an hour, it was a hard earned victory.

"It was probably not the most brilliant performance from myself or my team," said Robbie Paul afterwards, "but we're happy to take the win."

Next stop for the Bulls was the weekend jaunt across the channel to Paris, who were still searching for their first home win of the season.

The Bulls arrived at their hotel just a short walk from the Charlety Stadium at lunch time on the Thursday in preparation for another Friday-night televised game. Within an hour of checking in, the squad had changed into training gear and strolled down the tree-lined boulevard to the impressive stadium. For an hour, they went through a few basic drills, ridding themselves of any stiffness. Steve McNamara was put through a tougher session than the rest, proving to the coaching staff that leg and shoulder problems that had forced him out of the Wigan game had finally cleared up. His return helped offset the loss of Sonny Nickle, who had taken a bad knock to an arm at Wigan that subsequent x-rays revealed was a hairline fracture and would need at least a month's rest. Nickle had been left behind, giving Nathan Graham a recall as eighteenth man.

After enjoying an evening meal together at the hotel, the squad piled onto the team bus for a sightseeing tour of Paris by night. It had been arranged by Elliott to prevent players breaking into small groups and wandering off in search of the attractions - or distractions - that Paris offered, or alternatively sitting around the hotel and becoming restless.

Not all the players were keen at first, but it proved to be a good move. The travel representative who had been appointed to look after the Bulls was a small, 40-something year-old bloke from London who knew nothing about Rugby League and spent the other 51 weeks of the year looking after pensioners on short breaks to Bournemouth. Handling the

The Bulls army of fans followed them across the Channel to Paris

Bulls was a whole new ball game for him, and it didn't take long for James Lowes to politely explain that they didn't need reminding that the French drive on the right, that the river was called the Seine and a cruise was a nice way of enjoying dinner, or that they should be tucked up in bed by 10 o'clock.

"Remember you have a game tomorrow and you must conserve your energy," said the courier, wagging a finger at the players as though he was addressing a kindergarten. Predictably it brought a hail of expletives, and he dug a bigger hole for himself when he churned out feeble attempts at jokes. Eventually Brian McDermott stepped forward, took the microphone and told the poor bloke to move aside. Or words to that effect.

McDermott soon had the bus in raptures. His colourful commentary was far more entertaining, and deserves a chapter in this book all to itself. Unfortunately, this book would then need an '18' certificate, so until McDermott decides to release a CD version, you'll have to rely on your imagination.

Further entertainment was provided by the double-act of Bernard Dwyer and Paul Loughlin. Both sat next to each other at the very front of the bus immediately behind the French driver who, unable to speak or understand a word of English, simply joined in the laughter coming from the back of the bus without realising he was the focus of the joke.

Eventually, after about an hour, the bus pulled up alongside the magnificent Paris Opera House and the players were allowed to have an hour to themselves. Little groups formed and headed off in all directions, mostly in search of food.

As eleven o'clock approached, the players regathered on the street outside the bus. A hundred yards down the road a small group of well-dressed men appeared. In the distance, they looked familiar. "I don't believe it," sighed Robbie Paul. "It's the directors. A city the size of Paris and we bump into the directors."

Sure enough, it was Chris Caisley and his fellow board members with a couple of sponsors. They had been for dinner at a nearby restaurant and spotted their players as they strolled past the window. For a few moments several players were unsure as to how they would react, but Caisley broke the ice with a few jokes and before long everyone was again in a jovial mood.

Caisley and his party headed off into the night in search of a suitable watering hole and the players boarded the bus back to the hotel, diverting via another McDonalds on the way.

Next day, the Bulls had a light run-out at a local university sports field before someone in a peaked cap decided to intervene and ushered the squad off the grounds despite the Bulls having prior permission to train there.

They say it's the sign of a good team when you play badly but still win. If that's true, the Bulls were about to prove they were very good side indeed. In what was probably their worst performance of the season, the Bulls maintained their unbeaten start but only after being given a mighty scare by PSG.

Twice, the Paris side clawed their way back to threaten a major blow to the Bulls' Super League ambitions before skipper Robbie Paul rescued his side with two late strikes.

The feeling amongst the small band of British journalists in the stadium that night was, that with perhaps the exception of their visit to Wigan , the Bulls had yet to get into gear, and were spluttering along as though their finely tuned engines were seriously misfiring. With just two games before their Wembley showdown against St Helens they needed to move out of neutral quickly.

Elliott admitted it was as though the clock had been turned back 18 months at times.

"It was well below what we are capable of," he stormed. "If we continue to play like this we're going to get our bottoms smacked pretty hard. We need to turn things around quickly, and Halifax on Wednesday offers us that opportunity. If we continue to flop around as we did tonight we'll be in big trouble."

But Elliott praised the Paris side, and predicted a bright future.

"They have the core of what could be a very good team. They need a couple more players who are capable of doing something special for them and breaking through a defence. But they work well as a unit. They will win a few games this year."

PSG had signalled their intentions within the first couple of minutes. Young scrum-half Matthew O'Connor, playing only his second game, nearly succeeded in putting his half-back partner Jeremy Robinson over, and prop Tony Priddle went desperately close with a powerful 20-metre surge.

But Steve McNamara popped over a simple penalty to open the Bulls' account, before Paul Cook intercepted from 65 metres as O'Connor lofted out a pass meant for his winger. McNamara added the goal, but Paris were enjoying the majority of possession and were far more fluent than the Bulls, who struggled to make forward progress until Glen Tomlinson and Tahi Reihana combined twice in quick succession after half an hour to create the position for James Lowes to burrow over from dummy half. Cook popped over the goal in the absence of McNamara who had been taken from the field, and, 14 points ahead, the Bulls appeared to have blown away the cobwebs.

But PSG finished the half strongly. Tomlinson's chip through caught the leg of Wayne Sing, who regathered and sent Jamie Olejnik sprinting in from 70 metres. Danny Peacock went close for the Bulls with a typically strong charge but, on the stroke of half-time, PSG turned on the style again in a frantic all-out assault. The ball passed through eight pairs of hands in a thrilling move covering some 50 metres, before finally allowing Olejnik to claim his second.

Cook regained the initiative for the Bulls after the restart with his second. but even though they were 18-8 ahead, the Bulls hadn't really offered much for their sizeable travelling support to justify an expensive trip across the channel.

PSG sensed this lethargic mood and again came back strongly. Tomlinson tried to inject some variety to the Bulls' attack, but his long pass was plucked out of the air by Robinson, who raced the length of the pitch to bring his side to within four points.

There was a carbon copy minutes later, this time Paul the culprit, as Deon Bird claimed the game's third interception try. Anthony Wall blew the chance of putting PSG ahead, but his side had the upper hand and were playing with confidence.

It led to the most exciting part of an otherwise dull game, as PSG pressed hard for that elusive home win, while the Bulls desperately tried to maintain their unbeaten start.

Referee John Connolly twice needed video assistance in a frantic final ten minutes as McNamara was held just short, and then Cook just failed to get a hand to Bradley's cross-field kick. Paul clinched the game with his quick double, the first after taking a pass from man of the match Cook after Bradley and Lowes had combined well.

The Bulls' faithful were still celebrating when two minutes later the Kiwi struck again, taking a pass 30 metres out and apparently running up a blind alley before shrugging off Olejnik and driving low through three would-be tacklers.

It secured a rather flattering 30-18 win, but left Elliott with plenty to ponder going into the final week before Wembley with games against Halifax and Sheffield. His only cause for satisfaction was that no more injuries had surfaced, and he would be able to pick from strength for the following Wednesday night's trip to Thrum Hall. Steve McNamara's troublesome shoulder was not causing too much concern, and Matt Calland's back problem that forced his late withdrawal just hours before kick-off in Paris was also clearing up.

"The players didn't invest enough either physically or mentally on Friday to have any worries about Wednesday," blasted Elliott.

But the player who rescued them in Paris wouldn't be around at Halifax. Immediately after the Paris game, Robbie Paul was whisked to Charles de Gaulle Airport for a flight to Sydney. He'd been selected to play for New Zealand against Australia in the special ANZAC Day Test, the first under the Super League banner and a game Paul was desperate to play in despite the best efforts of the Bulls to persuade him to stay in Britain to prepare for Wembley.

"I didn't need an alarm clock to wake me up," laughed Paul. "After all, I hadn't been to bed. I caught the Air France flight to Heathrow at 7.45am thinking how much easier my Bradford team-mates would have it with the relatively short trip home to the north of England.

"I flew Singapore Airlines to Australia. No frills, down the back with the real people. I found myself between two old folk. They were ready for a long chat, but I wanted some kip. A sleeping pill knocked me out for most of the trip to Singapore.

"The crew were great. They had all the latest movies, but I'd seen most of them because I am a movie freak, going to all the new releases. There were also some great video games.

"On the trip to Sydney I sat next to a South African businessman who had problems with missed flights. He'd been on the go for 36 hours, and he still had a couple of hours before he made it to his hotel in Brisbane. It made me feel a bit better.

"I arrived at the Holiday Inn at Coogee, a seaside suburb in Sydney, in the early evening. I was the only Kiwi. The rest of the side wasn't due to arrive until the following day. Not that it mattered. I crashed out.

"I awoke around 4.30am and watched the sunrise over the ocean for the first time in about four years. It was a spectacular sight. The Pacific Ocean which leads into the Tasman Sea. On the other side of the Tasman is New Zealand. I sat back quietly thinking about what was going to happen on Friday night. I would be playing for my country for the first time. My childhood dream come true. I've been sitting in the hotel thinking 'Here I am on the eve of the two biggest games of my life. My first Test - and a week later Wembley. Individually, I performed well at Wembley last year. The Lance Todd Trophy and £10,000. But I would have gladly given up both for a

Immediately after playing in Paris, Robbie Paul flew to Sydney to join the New Zealand squad

Cup-winner's medal. I've been blessed with the opportunity for a second chance. And I'm going to grab it.

"A Test win? A Wembley win? What a double that would be."

While Robbie prepared to meet Australia, back in Britain the Bulls had a real test of their own. Games against Halifax are always eagerly awaited by fans of both clubs. The villages of Shelf and Northowram on the main road connecting Bradford with Halifax are populated by supporters of both teams and, twice a year, neighbours become rivals. No-one wanted to face their workmates and rival supporters the following morning if their side had lost.

Leading up to the game, the Bulls announced a new arrival. Depleted of forward strength becuase of injuries to Sonny Nickle, Jeremy Donougher and Warren Jowitt together with the suspension of Brian McDermott, Matthew Elliott had been searching for a second rower. During the Paris weekend he had revealed that he was speaking to former Wigan and Leeds second rower Mike Forshaw and would conclude the deal on his return to England.

Forshaw had been playing for Saracens after becoming disillusioned with life at Headingley, but jumped at the chance to return to Rugby League with the Bulls.

" Saracens had seen me playing for Leeds on television and made a tentative enquiry. They asked if I would be interested in playing for them and I accepted because I was disappointed with Leeds attitude. Once I knew they were prepared to let me go it was a quick decision. Perhaps it was too quick because I never settled. I was so grateful to Matthew when he came in for me. I always knew I had the ability, it was just a matter of getting a start and someone showing confidence in me.

"I'd followed the Bulls on television and it was a dream move."

Within hours of signing, Forshaw was named on the bench for the Halifax game. It was a game that lived up to the pre-match hype. Relentless and tight, the Bulls emerged 28-26 winners to move back to top spot in Super League and celebrated by going for a midnight dip!

Within minutes of the end of the pulsating derby the battered troops were shipped onto a bus and ferried to a local swimming pool to begin their rehabilitation for the next game against Sheffield Eagles. It was another sign of the increasing professionalism that enveloped the whole club.

When the Bulls finally lifted the Super League title, Halifax at Odsal on a Wednesday night was one of the games they would look back on and realise the victory was one of the most crucial in the championship

Former Halifax winger Abi Ekoku tackled by his old club.

campaign. Down 28-16 midway through the second half, Halifax, led superbly by skipper Karl Harrison, scored two tries in ten minutes to bring them within two points of the Bulls with just nine minutes remaining.

In the dying seconds they had their chance to take the points after Harrison had jarred the ball from dummy half Abi Ekoku with a bone-crunching tackle on the Bulls 20 metre line. From the scrum the Blue Sox stretched the Bulls one way and then the next. But, with the Bradford line inviting, a misunderstanding between sub Craig Dean and the outstanding Mike Umaga ended with the ball on the floor.

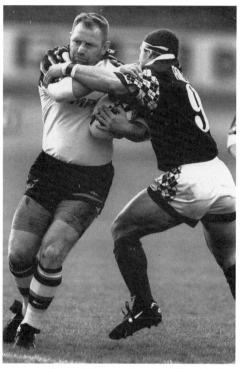

Bernard Dwyer takes the ball up during the thrilling win against Halifax.

It was a thrilling end to a brilliant match, played in cold blustery conditions and enjoyed by every one of the 13,285 spectators at Odsal.

The Bulls were without a string of star players - Donougher, McDermott, Nickle, Medley, Spruce and of course, Robbie Paul.

Halifax quickly had their own setbacks, when Kelvin Skerrett broke an arm in the very first minute and was joined in the dugout by Tongan Asa Amone, with a suspected broken collar-bone. But the Bulls held the trump cards in regulars Bernard Dwyer, James Lowes and skipper in the absence of Paul, Graeme Bradley.

Lowes, in particular, was magnificent, taking the right option every time at dummy half and creating four tries with his creative thinking. And one of the stand-ins, Cumbrian Simon Knox, couldn't have done much more, scoring a try hat-trick with his pace and strength. He opened the scoring in the second minute when he supported a huge break from Paul Anderson - fully fired up against his former club - to go in under the posts.

A Bradley grubber was scrambled dead three minutes later before the Blue Sox got back into the game.

Prop Wayne Jackson - on for Skerrett - was the man who did the damage when he sucked in Glen Tomlinson and Matt Calland before releasing a pass, which bounced along the ground for winger Damian

Munro to speed 20 metres for the try. Pearson couldn't convert and the Bulls stretched their lead when Dwyer forced Chris Chester to spill the ball with a huge hit just inside the Halifax half. The ball was spun wide and Lowes found Calland who shot in from 20 metres. McNamara converted from the right touchline.

The Blue Sox took their chance to come back again though Martin Moana. The Samoan hit Tomlinson with a massive tackle, forcing him not only into losing the ball, but leaving him dazed in the defensive line out in the centres. Pearson spotted the weakness and ran at the Aussie, brushing him aside on the way to the line. Tomlinson hobbled off as the Blue Sox upped the tempo.

They could have snatched a half-time lead when Paul Cook spilled a bomb in front of his own line and had to hack the ball dead as Bouveng threatened to pounce. And Abi Ekoku, another ex-Halifax man, had to use all his 6ft 4 inches to reach and defuse another Wayne Parker bomb.

Quickly it was back to the other end as Knox's pass just failed to reach Bradley, who had put him clear with a nice short ball. The 12-10 score reflected the end to end nature of a frenetic first forty minutes and little changed after the break. Moana stepped and went 40 metres down the middle of the park, and Jon Scales took Parker's chip to ease the pressure.

Then, after Halifax penned the Bulls in their own half, Bradley ran on the sixth tackle, put Calland away down the right, and he looped a pass inside for Lowes to send Knox on the way to the right corner for a spectacular score.

Umaga was the next to go through the middle, ignoring Knox's attempted tackle on half way. When Umaga found Rowley on his inside, the hooker looked all on the way a scorer, but astoundingly Knox was back to tackle him from behind and Rowley spilled the ball. It could have been the turning point, even though McNamara missed a penalty soon after, but the Blue Sox got the try they deserved when Moana picked the ball up from the base of the scrum, sprinted 20 metres down the blind side and sidestepped Danny Peacock to go under the posts.

Then, not for the first time, James Lowes created some daylight for the Bulls. From dummy half, he dabbed through a little grubber and, though blocked, McNamara was the first to the ball for a six-pointer.

Four minutes later, Lowes kicked again on the last tackle, this time on halfway, and followed through to collect, beating Umaga to the ball. His pass put Knox away on a footrace to the line. He won, sidestepping the covering Munro on the way. McNamara's goal made it 28-16 and Halifax should have been dead and buried. But back they came to set up that nailbiting finish.

"Our teams sure make close matches," said a relieved Matthew Elliott. "It was a game with quite a few turning points. You could not pick out one individual incident. We have a stronger outfit than last year but, as that game showed, Super League is a tougher regime. There are a lot of vastly improved teams and Halifax is one of them.

"I was pleased for Simon Knox who took his chance really well. But our win was down to three outstanding individuals, Bradley, Lowes and Dwyer. Take any one of those out and we'd have lost the game. Lowes was on the top of his game and the options he took, particularly on the last tackle, were a credit to him."

Simon Knox enjoyed his finest game of the season against Halifax, scoring a hat-trick of tries.

Knox made sure he kept the match-ball after scoring his first hat-trick for the Bulls but, as well as his points-haul, he remembered the game for the outstanding tackle that denied Halifax hooker Paul Rowley an almost certain try eight minutes into the second half.

"I'd missed Mike Umaga earlier on and I knew I had to make up for it," said Knox.

"I went chasing back and I managed to come up with a forced error. It was a wonderful feeling of relief when the ball came loose."

Knox paid tribute to coach Elliott and the departed Brian Smith for plucking him out of relative obscurity in the second division.

"I owe a lot to both of them for giving me the chance. The coach keeps telling me to back up James Lowes and Matt Calland and it sure paid off tonight. The first try came off a great break by Paul Anderson and the second was down to both Calland and Lowes.

"James is an excellent player, a model professional with a good rugby brain. He's everything you'd want from a hooker and he is guaranteed to make some breaks every game. You have to make sure you go with him.

"My third try might be put down to the luck of the bounce when Lowesy kicked through, but he has done that a few times so it can't just be luck. Once again he read the play brilliantly and luckily I was in support."

Knox knew that even with this match-winning performance behind him it wasn't enough to guarantee a start at Wembley.

"Brian McDermott and Sonny Nickle will both be in contention for Wembley and they are both awesome players, but I am just delighted to be at Bradford and I'll take what comes."

Knox had another chance to clinch a Wembley place four days later when Sheffield Eagles visited Odsal. Again injuries were piling up. Casualties from the Halifax game were Paul Loughlin and Glen Tomlinson, but both played through the pain barrier, and flu-victim Danny Peacock, who started on the bench against Halifax, was back at centre.

Brian McDermott returned after serving his four-match suspension, Stuart Spruce resumed at fullback in place of Paul Cook and Paul Medley's shoulder problem responded well enough to allow him a place amongst the substitutes.

Elliott also thought about using Robbie Paul off the bench but, having arrived back from Test duty on the morning of the match, eventually decided against the idea.

Sonny Nickle was still suffering from the arm injury he copped at Wigan, but, desperate to win a place at Wembley, took his place in the back row.

The Bulls final shakedown before Wembley ultimately proved easier and less troubled than any of their other encounters since the punishing Cup semi-final against the Rhinos, although for 40 minutes they made hard work of a Sheffield side crippled by injuries to key players.

The second half was a stroll, following a sensational early breakaway try, with three more scores in a four minute spell finally breaking the Eagles' resistance.

And for the first time in weeks, Elliot delighted in reporting a clean bill of health. Apart from broken leg victims Jeremy Donougher and Warren Jowitt, he could choose a Wembley squad from all his eligible players.

"The way we played in the second half was great," said Elliott. "It reminded us of what we are capable of - we've finally got the horse in front of the cart, and, with a few people whipping it, it ran away today."

In the early stages it looked as though it would be all too easy for the league leaders, when left winger Abi Ekoku latched onto a clever Graeme Bradley pass to score his first try for the Bulls. Not content with one, Ekoku scored again after 15 minutes, this time feeding off Stuart Spruce's opportunism in picking up a loose ball near the corner flag.

Steve McNamara curled over one conversion and, with just a Mark Aston penalty in reply, the Bulls seemed set to cruise to their eighth straight league win at 10-2.

Several times the Bulls could have extended their lead but failed to translate their territorial advantage into points, too often falling down in the last quarter. The Eagles clawed their way back into contention through a mesmerising David Mycoe run and touchdown, when hardly a Bradford hand was laid on him. Aston goaled, then added a penalty in front of the posts, to level the scores at 10-10.

The Bulls huffed and puffed for a while until Bradley, having the latest in a succession of big games, forced his way through to restore the Bulls' lead.

Ekoku was denied a first half hat-trick when he was held over the line on his back, but Danny Peacock forced his way over just before the break.

The second half was largely one way traffic. A typical surging Paul Medley run almost instigated an early try in the corner and, moments later, Paul Cook picked up an Aston kick on his own line and sprinted diagonally through all but one of the Eagles team before handing on to Sonny Nickle, who outpaced full-back Lynton Stott over the remaining 40 metres to score.

Spruce released Bradley for a try just after the hour, before Paul Anderson got in on the act with two more touchdowns in the space of four minutes - also his first for the Bulls. McNamara converted all three on the way to a personal tally of seven goals.

James Lowes pounced to charge down a badly timed kick from Aston to allow McNamara to score and Peacock, whose workload was conspicuously high, side stepped his way through to send Brian McDermott, sporting a new and severely short hair cut, over for the tenth try.

Now, all eyes turned to the twin towers of Wembley.

6

GREAT EXPECTATIONS

BUOYANT from the drubbing of Sheffield Eagles that meant they would return to the twin towers as undefeated leaders of Super League after eight games, the Bulls' were relaxed and quietly confident when Wembley week finally dawned.

One of the disadvantages of the switch to summer League is that the Challenge Cup, traditionally the climax to a long season, is now effectively a pre-season competition whose final interrupts the Super League just as it gathers pace.

There is also a longer than usual wait between the semi-finals and the big day itself. St Helens had to wait six weeks, the Bulls five, and both could be forgiven for allowing themselves to become distracted from the chase for the biggest prize of all, the Super League title.

Indeed, Saints slipped up at Leeds, but the Bulls' firmly pushed aside any thoughts of their attempt to gain revenge on Saints to continue their ruthless charge to the top.

"It's got to be a good thing," reflected Elliott, relaxing with a beer in the Players Bar after the Sheffield win.

"We set out to win every match and to achieve everything we set out to do so far this season is great. Some of the performances haven't been too hot and we expect more of ourselves."

Even though he had tasted the Wembley experience twelve months earlier, Elliott was still trying to understand why British fans placed so much emphasis on the Challenge Cup. He, like most other Australians, feels the Championship is a far greater reward and a true measure of a club's ability.

"Wembley is in a bit of a bubble, in that whatever happens before and after seems to be forgiven as long as you win," he reasoned.

"It's that kind of competition where the fans place a lot of importance on just one game. I'm looking forward to the event rather than what kind of record we carry into the game."

But even he admitted to being swept along on the wave of emotion and expectation that was growing by the day. In his first season as head coach of Britain's fastest growing and most talked about side, the rookie had yet to taste defeat.

"At a personal level I occasionally take time out to think about what has happened over the last few months. Sometimes I catch a look at myself and think, wow!

"But with the demands of the job you don't get much time to reflect. I've always worked long hours and now my level of responsibility is higher, it is even more consuming. Even when I'm not at work I'm thinking it. There hasn't been anything unexpected about the job, but it is tough. It was always nice last year for me to recognise a problem or situation that needed to be addressed but let someone else deal with it."

That 'someone else' was of course Brian Smith, but by now the Bulls were very much Elliott's team.

"The whole club set-up is fantastic, but in particular my immediate staff have provided me with professional and personal support. We Rugby League people live in a pretty small community and sometimes you need to lift your head up and see what else is going on in the real world."

Preparation for the game began in a low key manner. All the players arrived at the Bulls' Rawdon Meadows training ground as normal on Monday morning and viewed the Sheffield game on video. Then it was out onto the field for a light session to "get a few toxins out of their muscles" according to Carl Jennings.

"I try to set a theme for each week, and this week will be no different," said Elliott. "You can't look at a game and go through each part of play explaining what particular skill needs to be executed because you're giving players too much information. On a gameday I guess I'm serious. That's how I was when I was a player. Some players like to joke about before a game, others sit quietly in a corner, others are bent double being physically sick. Everyone treats gameday differently.

"I'm not a coach who likes to have a clipboard out or pieces of paper. I've developed little processes for myself and sometimes when we have our pre-match meeting I'll use prompt-notes to refer to, but that's all. I like to talk to every player individually. I probably say too much to be honest because by gameday everything should be done.

"I make myself go out of the dressing room before a game so I'm not talking continually. I have a breather and sometimes Mick Potter tells me to stay out. He'll say, don't worry, let them go, you've done all you can."

Wembley week begins with a raid on kit supplier Mitre's factory

After training finished, it was time for one of those extra tasks that served to illustrate this was no ordinary week. The 25-strong top-squad piled into the two Bullmobiles and made their way to the Huddersfield headquarters of Pentland Sports - better known to Bulls' fans as Mitre.

Greeted by the now usual throng of TV cameras and press photographers, each player was presented with personalised holdalls packed with various goodies essential to any Wembley trip.

Training gear, shell suits, baseball caps, t-shirts, sweatshirts, polo shirts - all embroidered with "Wembley 1997" and the growing number of sponsors' logos.

New boots and trainers in a variety of colours were also eagerly snapped up and, of course, there was the exclusive new playing kit.

Graeme Bradley had brought along his young son, who quickly found his way into the showroom lined with hundreds of pairs of training shoes. An obliging Mitre salesperson soon had Bradley junior fitted out with the very best on offer.

Thirty minutes later, and the raid was over. The overladen Bullmobiles headed back to Odsal, leaving the Mitre organisation severely depleted of stock.

The next day, Elliott and his staff began to wind things up a little.

"We're getting more focussed on Wembley now. We'll do our last bit of conditioning and strength work before meeting the media this afternoon."

Elliott was referring to the customary team photo and informal chat with the hordes of reporters, photographers, television and radio people, all desperate for their own 'exclusive'.

It had been switched at late notice from Rawdon Meadows to Odsal, leaving no time for Peter Deakin to prepare the slick presentation the hacks had become accustomed to. Instead journalists and photographers began a free-for-all, chasing players into any suitable corner of the two dressing rooms or corridor once the Wembley squad picture had been taken in front of the main stand.

As usual, Robbie Paul was top of everyone's wanted list. Every photographer wanted a slightly different pose, each reporter searched for a different angle. Motorcycle couriers hovered anxiously in the background waiting to whisk video tape back to the studio for the evening news bulletin.

Most were content with the standard questions, mostly about his hat-trick last year and the effects of his journey around the world. Although every reporter asked almost identical questions, they all wanted to do it individually, one-on-one, as though Robbie was going to tell them a huge secret.

One persistent feature writer from the Daily Star trapped him for the best part of an hour, attempting to delve deep into his personal life. She was so protective of her story that she locked Robbie in the dressing room out of ear-shot of any prying competitors, much to the annoyance of other journos with fast approaching deadlines.

Elliott was bemused by the proceedings.

"It's a great part of the job. If every player or coach is honest with themselves they will agree that the media attention is part of the attraction for them doing this job.

"It's important that it doesn't become too much of a distraction though. I'll be glad when it's out of the way so we can fully concentrate on Saturday."

Eventually, shortly after seven o'clock, the final interview wound up and the players dispersed.

As usual, Wednesday was the players day off, but Elliott and his coaching staff spent the day reviewing videos and stat' sheets, going over everything in minute detail. On his desk lay copies of the team picture taken the previous afternoon. Every member of his top-squad was on show, resplendent in the new bright amber shirts. Even new signing Mike Forshaw, yet to play a game and cup-tied, was included.

But most of the others were eligible - and that meant one heck of a selection poser.

"Sleepless nights have become a regular occurrence for me lately!" said Elliott, casting a glance at the picture.

"I haven't settled on a final line-up yet and when I do get down to seventeen there's then the problem of how we're going to use them. There are two ways of looking at it. You can name the team on Monday and then have them thinking about it all week, or you can wait until the last minute and not give them enough time to prepare.

"I'll name the side tomorrow afternoon (Thursday), just after we get to our hotel. I think that is just about right for everyone. There isn't anything to be gained from playing mind games with Shaun McRae (St Helens coach). He will know roughly what my team will be just as I know what to expect from him.

"One of the less pleasant jobs you have as a head coach is to tell some people they are going to miss out. My view is that no matter what the result the whole squad will have contributed to it. The thing they must remember is that this isn't the last final that this club will be involved in. There will be other finals and other big games in the future, and if they miss out on this one they have to ensure they are selected for the next.

"For most people success is winning silverware, but there are other factors. At Bradford we have attracted crowds of 15,000. That has become the norm and to me is success because it is more than double what the club was achieving 18 months ago. We also provide great entertainment. That's a success.

"But on the playing side our ambition is to win every game we start. If we do that we'll get the results and accolades and trophies that come with it. It frightens me to look too far ahead. It takes your mind off what needs to be done every day at training. It's not just showing up and playing. A half hour session can take many hours of planning and preparation."

It was dark outside by the time Elliott left his office and headed back towards the family home at Bramhope.

His wife, Karen, was patiently waiting. After dinner, they allowed themselves for the first time to look ahead to the weekend.

"I'm going to make an effort to soak up the atmosphere as much as I can," Elliott said.

"I hope I will get many more opportunities to go to Wembley, but this is the 100th final and my first as head coach. I want to enjoy the occasion as best I can, but I coach best when I am totally focussed in on the event.

"I'm not a dour person but I guess when I'm on the sidelines concentrating during a game I must look that way. People will probably say I'm not enjoying myself, but that's my style and how I need to be.

"I always try to get up in the stands to have an elevated look at what's happening. With Nobby in the dugout and Mick running on the field it's like having three different perspectives so that we can pool information and make changes as necessary.

"Karen is coming down on Friday with the girls. My youngest is two and is only just getting an understanding of what's going on. My eldest, Mia, is a Bulls' nut and totally into it. Lucy, my middle daughter, loves coming to Odsal but is a little laid back.

"I'll be so proud to have them with me. Karen has gone through a lot. She went through the highs and lows of seeing me play in a Grand Final and then ending my career early because of injury. I was never someone who was an immediate selection every week, and I did my fair share of reserve-grade games, but she has always been there for me and it's nice for her to be part of this weekend."

Elliott felt he had done all in his power to get a Bulls win, but he wasn't happy with circumstances outside his sphere of control.

"Ever since the semi-final I haven't been able to put the amount of preparation into games that I would like. There hasn't been any rhythm because the games have been piling up. I've been trying to get a feel of which players are struggling, who needs a rest, who's going to shake off that niggling injury.

"But it wouldn't be any fun if it was easy. There could be a few less obstacles if the fixture planners did their jobs better. I think the best example of that was the Castleford game in midweek after the semi-final. We won but that was about all. It lacked something.

"Rugby League is played with aggression and if you don't plan your fixtures well you taint the sport. There are some tough decisions to be made. The sport is on the brink of something special if those decisions are made. It will hurt a lot of people and it will challenge tradition, but I believe we have an opportunity now to make a great game for the future."

The following morning, outside the Novotel just off the M606, a small crowd of enthusiastic well-wishers had gathered along with the mandatory throng of TV crews and reporters.

There, too, were the injured and fringe players who would travel south with the sponsors, VIPs and players' wives the next day.

Inside, the mood was calm and cheerful but at the same time quite tense. In just a few minutes all the hanging around would be over and the party would be on their way.

The players had subconsciously begun the countdown to 2.45pm on Saturday. Some sat quietly sipping orange juice, some paced up and down casting anxious looks at their watches. Others gave interviews to the press or chatted outside to the fans.

Paul Cook and Nathan Graham had a game of pool, Brian McDermott cracked a few jokes.

The Bulls arrive at their luxurious St Albans base.

Gary Tasker went through the carefully thought out itinerary, and realised the team's tour bus was late. A hurried phone call to the offices of Wallace Arnold soon rectified that, but suddenly a major problem surfaced.

James Lowes had woken up with an abscess in his upper mouth, and by the time he arrived at the hotel he was in a lot of pain.

Anxious to keep such news away from the media, the late arrival of the bus turned out to be a blessing in disguise. Lowes was bundled out of a back door, into a car and taken for emergency treatment at the club's dentist in Brighouse, while the cameras focussed on the eventual arrival of the bus and the process of loading up all the kit and supplies.

Shortly after 11.00am, an hour late but with Lowes safely back on board, the bus made its way up the sliproad onto the M606, merrily sounding its horn at the small band of supporters waving them off.

The team's headquarters for the next two nights was the Sopwell House Hotel and Country Club, hidden away down a narrow winding lane in the leafy suburbs of St Albans.

Last year, the Bulls had stayed south of London but, having endured a four hour journey to Wembley for the Friday walkabout session, had decided against using the same base again.

"We got most things right last year except the ride to the stadium which was a joke," recalled Elliott.

"This time we are half-an-hour away with terrific facilities on hand. It will be good for the players to be in this environment and just emphasises what a special event they are participating in."

Gary Tasker plumped for Sopwell House because of its unbeatable references from various sporting organisations. Many soccer teams regularly stay there, including England. Holland used it as their base for Euro '96, and Great Britain's Rugby League team had stayed there before the 1992 World Cup Final. Whilst the Bulls were in residence, Arsenal and Sheffield Wednesday also turned up.

It was an idyllic setting, but it seemed strange to see the burly Bulls wandering around the grounds in just a pair of shorts whilst well-to-do forty-something women arrived in BMWs and Mercedes for a mid-day work out at the exclusive health farm. The hotel staff were obviously well versed in dealing with soccer and rugby teams, and had allocated the Bulls their own dining room and video suite well away from other guests!

Once the formalities of checking in had been completed, the players wandered the grand corridors flanked with polished wood panelling in search of their sumptuous rooms. Along the way, some of them paused to study the numerous framed and signed shirts that proudly boast of previous guests. Amongst the dozens of international soccer shirts the Bulls eventually found what they were looking for. Hidden away down a narrow corridor that leads to the gent's toilet is the Rugby League collection. Not many - only half a dozen, but well worth a few minutes, and even a photo for the family album.

Pride of place goes to a fully signed and elegantly framed England shirt from the 1995 World Cup. Paul Cook was in that squad and remembers his stay at Sopwell House fondly. He's quick to point to his signature.

There are also a couple of Wigan shirts from their numerous Wembley visits, and a Great Britain one from the 1994 Ashes series. By the end of the weekend, a Bulls shirt would also hang there, displacing an unfortunate but snazzy little offering from Great Britain men's hockey team.

Within an hour of checking in, the team boarded the bus again. Training was planned for late afternoon at nearby fields, about a fifteen minute drive away. James Lowes took his usual position in the courier's seat at the front, and amused the troops with witty remarks via the microphone.

But no-one was joking as the bus pulled onto the training fields. Someone had forgotten to pre-warn the Bulls that a local school was

Glen Tomlinson, Danny Peacock, Carl Jennings, Paul Medley,
Steve McNamara and Simon Knox take a break.

holding its annual sports day, and had already occupied much of the
level field and running track.

A cricket match was well underway at the other end, leaving only a
public park for the Bulls to step up their crucial preparation. Elliott was
not amused.

Patience wearing thin, he paced the length and breadth of the park,
attempting to create something resembling a pitch with marker cones.
The players went through their warm-up routines before Noble and
Potter began to run a few defensive drills.

A small but inquisitive crowd soon developed, but Elliott was
reluctant to continue with the session for fear of a player twisting an
ankle on the many ruts and bumps. It might be good enough for Arsenal

The Bulls stretch out having eventually found a suitable training pitch at St Albans.

to knock a ball around on, but this was the Bulls!

"We can't do anything here," Elliott sighed to Peter Deakin with a shake of the head.

Deakin immediately dialled back to base on his mobile, and asked the hotel to suggest an alternative venue.

Overhearing the conversation, two men stepped from the growing crowd of on-lookers. They introduced themselves as physical education teachers from a large school a few miles down the road and readily offered the use of their facilities.

The Bulls climbed back on board the bus and set off in pursuit of a decent training ground with the school teachers leading the way.

Turning into the school, Elliott was a happy man. Huge, flat, well-mown lawns stretched as far as the eye could see. There were even a couple of rugby pitches - with posts!

The group split in two and Elliott's support staff began the routine of drills once more. Elliott himself was a lone figure, marching between the two groups before pausing to gather his thoughts. Suddenly, everyone was switched on. The joking stopped, the sunglasses were put away, the personal stereos switched off. The light-hearted banter was replaced with intelligent analysis of different plays, and code-names to call highly complex moves.

After an hour, Elliott appeared reasonably pleased. He allowed an occasional smile, and even clapped when a new move he had introduced was eventually mastered.

At this point, 48 hours before the game, he still hadn't decided on which seventeen would walk out at Wembley. All week he had fielded calls from the media, anxious to get the exclusive news, but he remained tight-lipped. Even his players weren't sure who was in and who was out.

As the session neared its end, he called his squad together and sat them down. They took on water and listened to his observations, some aimed at specific individuals, some aimed at the whole group.

Then he read out thirteen names.

"You guys get set to receive the ball, the rest form up as the opposition," he shouted.

It is the first hint at what his Wembley side might be. Glen Tomlinson, who had started every Super League game leading up to the final, was on the sidelines along with Nathan Graham, Paul Medley, Matt Calland and Simon Knox. They try to laugh and joke, but each knew that a place on the bench was going to be the best they could expect.

But even then, Elliott played his cards close to his chest, and for the final fifteen minutes of the session switched things around to allow Tomlinson to call the shots.

By seven o'clock, the squad were tucking into a mountain of pasta and fresh fruit, and guzzling gallons of specially prepared isotonic drinks. After a brief team meeting, they had the remainder of the evening to themselves.

It was interesting to see how different players dealt with the pressure that was building up. Some went for a swim, several decided on a massage. Others simply returned to their rooms for a quiet night.

But a small group decided to commandeer the team bus and head off to a huge bowling alley at Hemel Hempstead. Two players keen to go emerged from showering themselves to see the bus disappear in a cloud of dust down the hotel driveway.

"I can't believe it. They've gone without us," a startled Tahi Reihana said to his room-mate and skipper Robbie Paul.

"That's because of you pampering yourself with CK1," laughed Robbie, who reinforced the point by turning up his nose and playfully blowing a kiss in Tahi's direction.

The pair call for a taxi and set off in pursuit of their buddies.

Meanwhile, in the hotel's plush bar, chairman Chris Caisley and his fellow directors prepared for dinner by teasing each other about the following day's much anticipated round of golf.

Later, during the meal and after several bottles of Chardonnay, the intense rivalry was further illustrated when it emerged that I had been dragged into this fierce battle of the greens by agreeing, quite innocently, to carry Colin Tordoff's, Jack Bates' and Gary Tasker's prized golf clubs

A nervous Tahi Reihana clowns about with Paul Cook, Nathan Graham and Sonny Nickle

in the boot of my car.

Caisley and the rest, who were to rely on hiring a set of clubs, were quite miffed when they learnt of this mischievous attempt to gain an unfair advantage. Fearing I was about to be banished to the stables for my part in this little plot, I swiftly downed the remains of my wine, made my excuses and retired for the evening.

The Friday walkabout is one of the highlights of Wembley week for any team. Each competing side is allocated a half hour slot to get a feel for the place. It's the first chance to see the famous old stadium, to walk on the hallowed turf and sit in the historic dressing rooms occupied by so many famous names of the past.

It's also the last chance for the media to grab the interviews and photographs that will make the Saturday morning papers. The last chance for the respective coaches to play mind games on their counterpart.

There was a special aura amongst the players as they donned their uniform white polo shirts adorned with sponsors logos and embroidered Wembley 1997 badging, and gathered on the hotel lawn.

There was near silence on the thirty-minute drive to Wembley. Radio One blasted out over the speakers but no-one was really listening. The players mostly stared vacantly out of the windows, deep in thought about the following day's game.

Soon, the famous outline of Wembley loomed on the horizon. A small band of autograph hunters were there to greet them and, after duly obliging, they made their way up the cavernous tunnel and out onto the pristine pitch.

Tahi Reihana was making his first visit to the stadium. "Awesome. Just awesome," he repeated several times.

Sonny Nickle took his trainers off. "This grass is better than my carpet," he laughed.

Brian McDermott responded in his usual witty way, going into great detail about the type of seed Wembley use and how long it takes to germinate. It was hard to tell whether Sonny was impressed or simply lost in bewilderment.

Danny Peacock appeared to be the most laid back - literally. He took his shirt off and simply sunbathed for thirty minutes.

The rest slowly walked around, taking pictures and recalling great moments from past finals.

James Lowes did a great impersonation of Gareth Southgate missing his penalty in the Euro '96 semi final against Germany. The round of applause was so impressive, he did it again in slow motion, using Steve McNamara as the goal-keeper. McNamara dived elegantly to the right, but quickly got to his feet when he heard a crunch. His £100 Ray Bans had been shattered beyond repair.

Amid the laughter, Matthew Elliott measured the width of the pitch and took McNamara's mind off his glasses by talking about the kicking options.

All too soon, the Bulls were asked to leave to allow St Helens their turn. The journey back to St Albans was a nightmare, London's roads choked with traffic thanks to a bomb scare.

Elliott decided on a short training session before tea, followed by the final team briefing and an early night.

Twenty-four hours later, the Bulls were back at Wembley. This time, there were thousands of fans lining the route for the last couple of miles as the team bus slowly picked its way through the throng.

7

No Place For Losers

ONE of the countless side attractions of the Challenge Cup Final was the developing battle between the top two hookers in the country. James Lowes and Keiron Cunningham would oppose each other knowing that the winner of this particular personal duel would take the early running in the race for a Great Britain place against Australia in November.

Both players are outstanding individuals, different in style perhaps but equally effective. The modern hooker's role, of setting up crucial plays in attack while in defence preventing the other side darting though from acting half-back had been mastered by both players.

Cunningham is said to have the edge on attack, but Lowes is the better defender, averaging over 30 tackles per match. Both players have the ability to commit defenders and then off-load in the tackle.

Speaking before the final, Cunningham heaped praise on his rival, making a surprise admission.

"James plays a more intelligent game than I do. I tend to play things of the cuff," he explained.

"He's an exceptional player who reads the game well, sets up plays from dummy-half, and is a distributor and organiser. He has more experience than me, but as I progress I hope to add some of the qualities of his game to mine.

"I tend to do what's necessary without any real idea why I do it. When I set off from dummy-half I am looking for a break through a possible half-gap, but it isn't really part of any game plan or pattern."

Despite Cunningham's modesty, Lowes was too clever to be drawn into playing mind games by repaying the compliments.

"I don't think of this game as merely a contest against Keiron," he said.

"When you are playing against another hooker you don't come face to face with him much. So it would be a mistake to personalise that particular battle. There are plenty of other good players on their side to think about."

But Lowes did concede he was probably playing the best rugby of his career, though, as always, he continued to grossly understate his ability.

"It's been going well for me this season, I can't really complain. I suppose I'm playing half decent. But then I've had good players and coaches around me ever since I first signed for Leeds, and particularly since I came to Bradford, so that's why I've improved," he explained before citing former Great Britain skipper and hooker Brian Noble as an example.

But he dismissed any thoughts that it was time for a hooker to win the Lance Todd Trophy, after a 37-year gap.

"When someone does something outstanding, like Robbie last year, they inevitably win it. I'm surprised, given the nature of the modern game, that no hooker has won the Lance Todd Trophy for so long, but I wouldn't expect any particular position to dominate the award.

"I'm not going out there to think about winning personal awards. I'll just work hard on my general all-round game without thinking that I'm going to top the tackle count, or trying to do as many doubles as I can, merely to look good on the stat's sheets. I don't think about stat's either before or after the game. It just isn't my style."

"Some people are allowing stat's to dominate their thinking and players naturally want to come out well in any stat's charts. No statistic ever won a Rugby League game, so I just try to do everything well."

Lowes was convinced of one thing however. The Bulls would be far stronger than the previous year when he had to sit on the sidelines cup-tied.

In addition to Lowes, the Bulls also had Stuart Spruce, Steve McNamara, Danny Peacock, Glen Tomlinson and Tahi Reihana to add flair, guile, consistency and solidity to a Bulls side that was so impressive in that narrow defeat twelve months earlier.

Lowes firmly believed that they were on the tide of an irresistible surge to a major trophy.

"I can remember everything about Wembley last year as a spectator," he smiled. "I'm sure it will be at least as good this year when I'm on the field. With what we learned last year we can take it one stage further."

While the media made much of the Cunningham and Lowes confrontation, another vital member of the Bulls team was preparing for the biggest game of his life.

When the Bulls made a commitment to become one of the biggest and best clubs in the world, part of their strategy was to build the strongest possible squad of players. One of their most inspired signings of recent

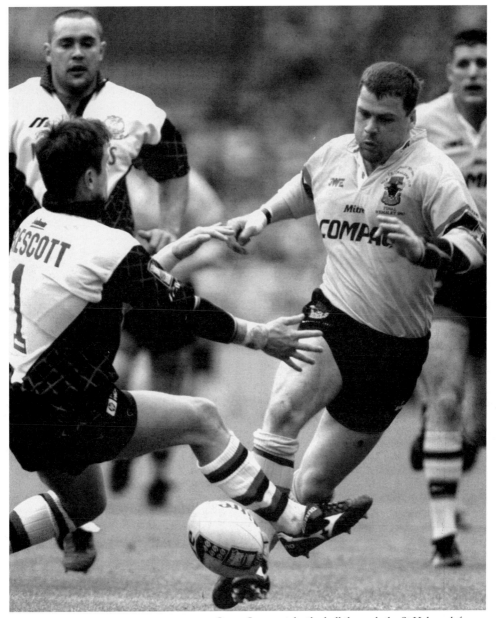

James Lowes stabs the ball through the St Helens defence.

years was that of centre Danny Peacock.

Unknown in Britain and unwanted in Australia, Peacock arrived at Odsal in January after a steady but unspectacular career with Wests, Gold Coast and South Queensland Crushers. His uncompromising style made him an instant hit with the Bulls fans, and he quickly became a key player in an impressive backline.

Now, he was about to achieve every player's dream.

"I've never known anything like it before," he said. "It's such a big occasion, and I'm looking forward to it immensely.

"Back home watching Wembley on TV every Australian dreams about one day playing there. I never thought I'd get the chance. It was one of the factors in deciding to uproot my family and come over here. The whole experience so far has been unbelievable, and we haven't even got to game day yet!

"We haven't played too well in a couple of games recently, but we talked it through last week. It worked for us, and on Sunday we began to show what we are capable of. That big win against the Eagles has given us a lot of confidence. We haven't played as well as we can, and we know we can do much better, but the signs have been there for the last few days that it's coming."

Peacock would be up against a former Bradford player, international centre Paul Newlove.

"Paul's a very good player but I like playing against the top players because it brings the best out in me. I'm going to enjoy playing against St Helens.

"They have a lot of pace and they have players who can bust the line and put people into holes, but so have we. We're prepared for it, and we are ready to put the work in to ensure we come away with the win. We haven't lost a game yet, and we don't intend losing this one.

"The blokes never stop talking about it. At lunchtimes, when everyone is normally quiet, one of the blokes will suddenly say something and everyone joins in, chatting about something to do with the weekend, asking questions and sharing information.

"Everyone is so focussed on one thing - winning the Challenge Cup."

As it turned out, for the second successive year St Helens destroyed the dreams of Bradford players and supporters. They clinched the Centenary Challenge Cup thanks largely to the clever half-back pairing of Tommy Martyn, who won the Lance Todd Trophy as man of the match, and the chief tormentor of the previous year, Bobbie Goulding.

It was a triumph of the matador's brains over the Bulls' brawn, as the precision of Goulding, the positioning of Martyn, and the pace of Anthony Sullivan triumphed over the Bulls power game.

Goulding and Martyn combined twice in the first half for scores which kept Saints in the game, at a time when the rampant Bulls looked like running away with it before Martyn set up second half scores for Chris Joynt and Sullivan to effectively settle it.

Last year's aerial bombardment of Nathan Graham, which won Saints the cup from a seemingly hopeless position, is now part of Wembley folklore.

Danny Peacock charges past Steve Prescott for a try

But with Super League's form full-back, Stuart Spruce, bolstering the Bulls' back door this year, Goulding took the low road to victory, sliding grubber kicks behind the defensive line for Martyn and Steve Prescott to chase.

The tactic worked twice for Martyn's two first half touchdowns, and sandwiched between them Prescott almost repeated the trick, only for Abi Ekoku to hack the ball dead at the last moment.

It was a pulsating first forty minutes that left the capacity Wembley crowd breathless. Martyn's first try in the ninth minute was almost against the run of play, as Bradford hit top speed from the whistle. They thought they'd scored as early as the third minute when Spruce out-jumped Danny Arnold to Steve McNamara's bomb, but knocked on in doing so.

McNamara was running the show for the Bulls, with James Lowes, as ever, driving the no-nonsense pack forward. It was McNamara who orchestrated Bradford's instant response to Martyn's try, dummying the try-scorer and sending Sonny Nickle stampeding down the right flank to offload to Danny Peacock whose strength saw off Prescott's despairing tackle.

A mistake by Karle Hammond gave Paul Loughlin the chance to put the Bulls ahead for the only time.

The former Saint used every inch of his considerable reach to intercept Hammond's pass, leaving Arnold and Derek McVey with no chance of catching him, and giving the Bulls' centre some hope of getting his first winner's medal in his fifth Challenge Cup Final.

Hammond almost made amends immediately, only to have the ball stripped from his grasp with the whitewash beckoning, leaving it to Goulding and Martyn to produce a carbon copy of the first try to level the scores at 10-all.

The Bulls attacked again, and the ever-threatening Peacock looked to be in for his second try to restore the Bradford lead, but somehow Anthony Sullivan knocked the ball out as the Australian was diving over.

The tackle that injured Robbie Paul's foot and forced him on to the sidelines for a lengthy spell.

As Matthew Elliott admitted afterwards, the Bulls didn't make the most of such opportunities.

"We didn't get the result today because of poor execution at crucial times," he said. "With a bit more control and composure, we had the opportunities in the first half to go in perhaps ten or twelve points in front."

With the hooter approaching, the 10-all deadlock looked a fair reflection of the first half, but Hammond caught the Bulls napping with a solo effort of great determination. Bernard Dwyer was the first to miss the loose-forward as he charged towards a posse of Bulls protecting the line. Spruce, McNamara, Lowes and Paul Medley all had hold of him, but they couldn't keep him out, as, miraculously, he managed to fall onto the line to ground the ball.

Even coach McRae admitted that his charges had not been the best side in the first half, and had been lucky to go in 16-10 up.

But within 20 minutes of the restart and, with Robbie Paul reduced to a virtual spectator, the red and white ribbons were again being tied on the handles of the old tin pot.

Martyn featured in the three crucial incidents which settled the fate of the silverware. First, he brought off a brilliant ankle tap to deny Peacock what looked a certain try after McNamara had again done the damage, ducking under two high tackles to create the chance. Ekoku got the ball, but then it was Paul Newlove's turn to pull off a try-saving tackle as he held the Bulls' winger inches short.

Then Martyn was instrumental in the two scores that put the game out of reach of the Bulls in the ten minutes during which Paul was on the bench trying to defy a painful foot injury.

It was Martyn who provided the pass from which Chris Joynt went 25 metres to score, scything though Brian McDermott and McNamara and beating Spruce's cover.

And it was Martyn's kickthrough from 40 metres out which Anthony Sullivan reached before Spruce to claim a try which should not have been awarded, as television replays showed beyond doubt that Sullivan failed to ground the ball.

Referee Stuart Cummings couldn't have been expected to spot it, but it was precisely the sort of incident the in-goal judge is there for and had Bulls fans bemoaning the lack of a big screen, now the norm at big Super League games.

With his side three scores behind, Paul limped courageously back onto the field, but not even he could pull this one out of the fire. Instead it was James Lowes - now a three times Wembley loser - who did most to try to turn the game around. It was his chip, chase and hack on which Glen

Tomlinson reached for a 63rd minute try and, three minutes from time, Lowes himself bustled past Martyn and Prescott for a touchdown.

But it was all too late for the Bulls, with the gap still ten points. The gap would have been even wider had Chris Morley's 66th minute effort not been disallowed. Referee Cummings controversially penalised Martyn for a fearsome Cumbrian throw, which loosened the ball from Ekoku's grasp, enabling Morley to scoot triumphantly over the line.

Elliott conceded that the best team won on the day, but took consolation in his assertion that "the best two teams in the northern hemisphere bar none played here today."

Andy Goodway, who would later in the season be named Great Britain coach, had his own views on the game.

"The turning point was when Robbie Paul went down injured," Goodway pointed out.

"St Helens scored the two tries that sealed it shortly after. Saints just fed off it.

"At times both teams looked too nervous to win the game, as though they were frightened of winning it. It might have been because they wanted to win it so much. They made errors because they seemed reluctant to take the game by the scruff of the neck.

"Goulding's kicking was just fantastic. Bradford were expecting much of the same as last year. We were all expecting loads of high bombs short of the line, and it was the change of tactic to put the kicks in along the floor to get the defence turning that did it.

"There were several key incidents in the early part of the second half besides Robbie getting injured. There was the tackle on Steve Prescott, after his run out of defence, that looked to be crucial. Then almost immediately after, Tommy Martyn just managed to tap Danny Peacock's ankle as he was going for the line. Up 'til then the pattern of the game was Saints going into the lead, and the Bulls coming back at them to score.

"It was incredible really. One team would keep the other penned in their own territory for three tackles, and then there would be a bust and either a chance or a score down the other end. It wasn't fantastic like last year, but it was a decent game, completely different in nature."

Goodway's comments continued to offer a revealing insight into how different coaches think.

"If there was one thing I'd have done differently to Matthew Elliott, and it's easy to make these decisions watching the game as a neutral, I'd have put Glen Tomlinson on earlier. The Bulls were going forward well and making a lot of ground, getting into the positions where they needed a good short kicking game. Tomlinson would have been able to toe-poke a few balls into the in-goal to up the pressure on St Helens.

"Bradford were two scores down before he had a chance to settle into the game. I would have changed tack a little before then. They missed a decent short kicking game. Steve McNamara put two dead.

"Because they were making so many yards there was no long kicking game from either team. They were playing in each others half's so much they didn't need to do it and that is why the short kicking game near the line was so important. That was the difference to me. At times, the Bulls were forcing the game, spilling too much ball.

"That is just the way that the Bulls play. They hit the line and then look for support. They feed off that. But if you make an error then, eventually, you are going to have to pay for it, especially against a team like St Helens."

Robbie Paul hobbles down the Wembley steps after collecting his losers medal

But Goodway agreed with every Bulls fan when it came to discussing Sullivan's controversial try.

"Sullivan's try was never a try. Then again Tomlinson's try was preceded by an obstruction and Chris Morley had a try disallowed which should have been given."

Another top coach, Phil Larder, also had sympathy for the Bulls.

"Bradford lost the final in the first half," he said. "I don't think you can play so much better than the opposition in the first half, as Bradford did, go in 16-10 down, and expect to win.

"Bradford did lots of things right. Steve McNamara was attacking Newlove's inside shoulder - he did it twice, first when he put Sonny Nickle away for Peacock's try, then when he almost put Peacock in himself early in the second half.

The Bulls started better and looked more relaxed than St Helens. They had way, way the better of the first half. They controlled the ruck and made easy yardage. They were very unlucky to go in 16-10 down."

Larder disagreed with Goodway about the Bulls kicking game however, and said he wouldn't have done anything much different.

"I probably wouldn't have done anything differently as a coach from Matthew. It's unfair to say the Bulls didn't have a kicking game.

"Matthew put faith in the players who are playing well. Steve McNamara's kicking game has been absolutely outstanding since he came back from injury, and James Lowes created a try from a short kick."

As the heartbroken Bulls trudged back to the dressing room, an elated Keiron Cunningham managed to find a moment to embrace James Lowes in the tunnel. "A lot of talk was made about the battle between myself and James Lowes and at the end of the day I feel we both made our own contributions to the game," he said to nearby journalists.

"I am a big mate of his, and I know he will be as gutted as I'm elated.

"It was just as tough as last year, but we were better prepared for what we had to do."

The journalists then turned to Saints winger Anthony Sullivan, and asked about his controversial try.

"I thought I got to the ball and got it down fairly, although it did all happen in a fraction of a second," he said.

"People were saying that I didn't ground it properly, but there were two officials as well as the referee, and they were all happy. I don't know why I should be worried. I have certainly gone in for more clear cut tries and had them disallowed, so I suppose they all even out over a season.

Bulls fullback Stuart Spruce echoed the feelings of his team-mates.

"It's one we should have won but Tommy Martyn and Anthony Sullivan managed to get round the back of us and grab tries that we really should have stopped.

"They scored at a crucial time just before half-time, and that meant that they came out for the second half on a big high. Their kicking game was excellent and, in the end, that was possibly the main difference between the two sides.

"We were expecting more high kicks, but we really should have the low ones covered too. It was a big disappointment."

Steve McNamara, slumped in the far corner of the Wembley dressing room, agreed with Spruce.

"This was worse than last year, because we really thought this was to be our year. Even though we had conceded that try just before half-time, I still thought we could have done it.

"It was a blow losing Robbie, but we should have had it won by then if we had taken what was on offer.

"Wembley is no place for losers."

The Bulls didn't hang around too long at Wembley. Though the players hadn't been told about it, a win-or-lose party had been arranged at the Heathrow Hilton hotel. All the players wives and girlfriends were there, along with sponsors and staff. Singer Anita Madigan, now a staunch Bulls fan and firm favourite with the Odsal crowd, sang live on stage and before long the players began to overcome the disappointment and get the smiles back on their faces.

One by one, the more adventurous in the audience dared to take the microphone and perform a duet with Anita, much to the delight of everyone else. Tahi Reihana and Robbie Paul won the impromptu karaoke session with a terrific version of "I Believe I Can Fly", but they were given a run for their money by Brian McDermott's "Kiss" and Paul Loughlin's "Wild Thing".

The party raged into the early hours, but early next morning the fleet of Wallace Arnold coaches were lined up outside to ferry the Bulls back up the M1 to Bradford.

Waiting for them outside the Town Hall were over 2,000 fanatical supporters. A stage had been erected and the Bullettes were entertaining them as they patiently waited for the homecoming. As losing finalists, not one Bulls player expected such a reception and were reluctant to board the open-topped bus at Odsal for the two mile journey into the city centre.

But as the bus made its way down Manchester Road, car horns sounded and people came out of houses and shops to wave at their heroes. By the time the bus turned into Centenary Square, the emotional players were genuinely shedding occasional tears.

"This is why this club is so special," said Robbie Paul with a lump in his throat. "What would they do if we won?," he asked.

It was less than 24 hours after the defeat, their first of the season. But, thanks to a strange quirk of fate, in less than a week they would have chance for revenge. The fixture planners had decided to send St Helens to Odsal for the resumption of the Super League campaign.

8

BACK TO BASICS

THE immediate days after the Challenge Cup Final tested the character of everyone connected with the Bulls. After the game, the critics rounded on the club despite them heading the Super League table. Cocky, loud-mouthed, brash - the Bulls got what they deserved, sneered their critics, and plenty of neutrals gloated on the sidelines. Now those critics were asking whether the Bulls could survive the disappointment of defeat.

The cock-a-hoop Saints headed for Bradford eight days after Wembley just two points behind the Bulls, eager to regain the initiative and take a massive step towards retaining the trophy they had won the previous season.

"We had a glorious chance last week but we blew it," shrugged former Saint Paul Loughlin as he prepared to meet his former side once again and forget about a new but unwanted record he had acquired. Five trips to Wembley - five defeats.

"Each time I have lost at Wembley I've felt just the same," he said. "Each match is a new experience, and each defeat is a new defeat. But it isn't cumulative, which is fortunate. Wembley is such a unique occasion, so it's easier to recover from than most other games that you lose. After the game you celebrate just because you were there.

"We came home and trained on Monday and Tuesday, and that's the best thing to do. We have already flushed the match out of our system. In any case I've never been one to mull over a defeat.

"We had plenty of chances to win the game, but it wasn't our day, although I was convinced we would win early in the game."

Loughlin still couldn't work out how Karle Hammond managed to score that try just before half-time that sent the Saints in with a 16-10 interval lead.

"It was a soft try. There were four tacklers who would normally have

Mike Forshaw forces his way over a try on his debut against St Helens.

put him down without any trouble. But perhaps they just left it to each other. It's a mystery."

"Now we are going for the Super League title. We know that we can beat St Helens if we can hit the form we're capable of. We can play just as well as we did last year when we won so well. We perform so much better at Odsal against the better sides."

Loughlin was enjoying a new lease of life since his move to Odsal, despite originally having doubts about the move.

"I've stayed injury free, I look after myself, and I've learned a lot from the coaching staff since coming to Bradford. I don't feel anywhere near the end yet. Look at Graeme Bradley, he's three years older than me but he's playing superbly. Going full-time has been a great move. It allows us to concentrate on skills, and lets us study the game much more. I'm sure it has helped me to extend my career."

Loughlin and the Bulls got the win they so badly wanted, a comprehensive 38-18 victory and savoured the sweet taste of revenge. Their six try to three success also gave the Bulls a vital four-point cushion over their arch rivals at the top of the Super League.

Matthew Elliott was predictably relieved to see his side come through the big test with flying colours.

"I don't want to sound arrogant but I feel I've got a team that can win every game it plays and that's why last week was such a disappointment," he said.

"Winning tonight is a big weight off everyone's shoulders, but we've got to remember that this was only the ninth match of a long Championship campaign."

The game kicked off amid an awesome and heavily partisan atmosphere generated by Bradford's biggest crowd of the season - the vast open terrace was closed well before the start.

Within two minutes of the start it was evident that lady luck had switched sides since their Cup Final encounter. Tommy Martyn collected a rebound from his own kick but his long pass to Anthony Sullivan was too high and bounced harmlessly into touch.

Steve McNamara slotted over a straight penalty kick to put the Bulls ahead and, shortly after, James Lowes switched the direction of play in front of the Saints posts for Bernard Dwyer to twist his way through four would-be tacklers to score his first try of the season.

McNamara goaled and memories of last year's 50-22 thrashing flashed through many onlookers' minds.

Goulding brought Saints back into the game, kicking a penalty and crafting a try for Anthony Sullivan, but the Bulls stepped up a gear and Glen Tomlinson sent Mike Forshaw racing through at speed. Forshaw, on his debut, showed terrific strength to go over by the posts and McNamara converted.

Then McNamara scored a superb individual try, sidestepping his way through the Saints defence from 40 metres. His try inspired the Bulls to come forward in waves and only desperate defence prevented them scoring again.

But Saints winger Danny Arnold was sin-binned for deliberate offside just before the break and, in his absence, the rampant Bulls ran in two more tries. At 32-6, there was no way back for the faltering champions, though they responded by throwing caution to the wind and came up with a couple of tries to narrow the gap to 14 points before Simon Knox added the Bulls' sixth try.

"The difference between this week and last week was that tonight we took our chances," said Graeme Bradley. "St Helens' first few kicks didn't come off and we grew in confidence after that.

"We were without Sonny Nickle and Robbie Paul, but the blokes who came in did terrific and the crowd support was fabulous."

St Helens' boss Shaun McRae almost conceded the title there and then.

"Bradford's four-point lead is a big one at this stage. I can't see them losing too many games, particularly at home with such a partisan crowd.

"We can't afford to lose any more games, but I'm confident we can still bounce back from this. My team performs at its best when under pressure. A lot of things Bradford tried at Wembley which didn't come off worked for them tonight."

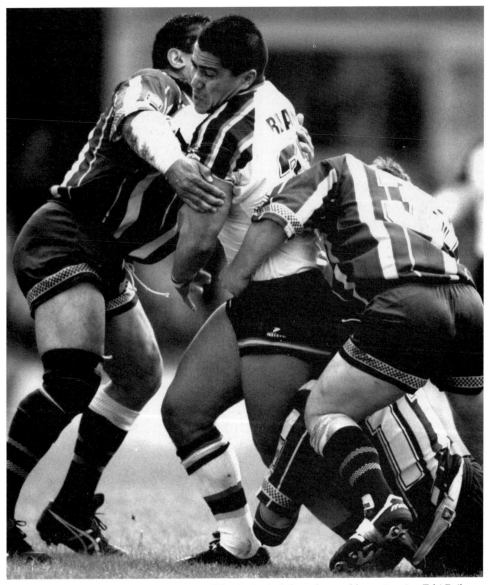

Warrington's defence has problems stopping Tahi Reihana

Next up for the Bulls was an away trip to Warrington. Robbie Paul's injured foot was still swollen but initial fears that he could be absent for the rest of the season had been dispelled. It was even hoped he would be able to make the Warrington game.

"He has progressed really well and is talking about being available on Sunday," said Elliott. "I think that might be asking a little too much, but we'll give him every chance."

In the end it was too much, and Paul had to accept he needed six weeks rest. His absence mattered not as the Bulls opened up a five- point gap at the top with a predictably powerful display against the beleaguered Wolves, running up a 38-14 win.

Warrington had all kinds of worries on and off the field, and their makeshift pack was never able to stand the tide as the Bulls six swept forward almost at will in the first 40 minutes. Matt Calland powered through early on, and Danny Peacock plucked a long pass from McNamara out of the air brilliantly to send big Paul Anderson galloping over.

The difference in class was amply illustrated a moment later when Graeme Bradley simply stepped through the home defence and found Mike Forshaw in support. Bradley's only dilemma was in deciding which of his four supporting teammates to send in for the try.

James Lowes took the direct route for another score, going himself from dummy half on the Warrington line to establish a 22-point interval lead. Peacock added another after the break, and Glen Tomlinson chipped in with a brace to confirm their superiority.

St Helens had dropped a crucial point at home to London on the Friday night to add to the Bulls' satisfaction.

"We were happy with the way St Helens went on Friday, but it was very important for us to come down here today and do well," said Peacock. "Warrington pushed us into a lot of errors late in the game.

"At 22-0 we were happy with our first half performance, but in the second half they really came at us. The last couple of tries really hurt us and no doubt we'll be taking a look at those tomorrow."

As Super League approached the half way stage, the Bulls were still unbeaten and Brian McDermott took time out to reflect on their achievements.

"The whole league has been levelled out and the power has definitely switched away from Wigan, and probably St Helens," he said.

"Last year Saints won a few games that really they shouldn't have. This year that has happened to us. We've played below par but come out with the win. To me, that's a sign of our strength just as it was for Saints last year.

"That's what makes a Championship side. Saints thoroughly deserved their title, but this year they haven't quite been up to the same level. Wigan, too, have lost a couple of games that perhaps in the past they would have won, but it just shows how close it is at the top. It's a reflection on how strong the competition is now in that whoever wins the title isn't going to do it by a massive margin."

"People might say we are favourites, but Saints won't agree and even though they are eight points adrift I wouldn't rule Wigan out of the race yet. There are twelve games left and there is still time for Wigan to come strong.

"Leeds are going well too. They've sneaked into second without anybody noticing and will have a big say in who wins the title. They could win it themselves - we have to play them home and away yet, and those two games will be massive."

Former Marine McDermott relished the tough competition and predicted that the Bulls will get stronger.

"The best teams now are the ones who put the effort in off the field. We do a hell of a lot of conditioning work at Bradford. After Wembley we were run ragged in the gym for a couple of days. Matthew is determined to ensure that if we do miss out on the title it won't be because of a lack of fitness.

"Some people in the media were trying to make an issue of the fact we allowed Warrington to come back at us in the second half last Sunday. They were saying that we lack the killer instinct that Wigan had, but that's nonsense. Wigan used to finish sides off early in the second half because of their superior fitness. They had seventeen superfit blokes playing against a bunch of part-timers. Other clubs fell by the wayside and allowed Wigan to trample all over them.

"That doesn't happen any more because clubs can now keep going for the full eighty minutes. That's what Warrington did to us. They came out fresh from the break and lifted their game again."

McDermott's thoughts then turned to the start of the World Club Championship, just two weeks away. The Bulls would open their campaign against the Penrith Panthers, and already there were suggestions that it might disrupt the Bulls machine that had thus far run so smoothly.

"The World Club Championship is going to be fantastic," he enthused. "I almost I wish I wasn't a player so I could sit back and watch all the games!

"It can work both ways for us. If we get great results against the Australian clubs we will come back a more confident side, and probably a more feared side. On the other hand, if we have a bad time we have to make sure we don't let it interrupt our league form. We showed with the way we bounced back after Wembley that we don't let defeats get to us."

Preparation for the next game, Oldham at Odsal, was disrupted by a shock development. Winger Paul Cook, never a regular but a favourite with the fans, signed for Huddersfield.

The Giants had been chasing the 20 year old goal-kicking winger or full-back for several weeks and the Bulls had finally been persuaded to release him. Agreeing to the transfer was tough for Matthew Elliott.

"It's the hardest thing I have ever had to cope with," he said. "It has affected me even more than the Wembley defeat, because I hold a deep affection for the kid.

"I have a responsibility to this organisation, and I have to do what is best for the long term interests of the club. I have to utilise the talent at my disposal to make ways for us to enhance our squad."

Cook put on a brave face, but was clearly shocked to find he was suddenly surplus to requirements.

"There are two ways of looking at it," he said. "I could have won the Super League and gone to Australia with the Bulls, or I could have spent the rest of the season in the reserves. Hopefully the Bulls will do well in Australia, and win the league too, but my future now is with Huddersfield. They have a lot of ambition and great facilities, so I hope it's one step back to make two forward."

In a shock move, Paul Cook was transferred to Huddersfield just days after playing at Wembley

Cook had made nine starts for the Bulls during 1997, scoring six tries. His last game was the Challenge Cup Final at Wembley before he was unceremoniously dumped into the Alliance team.

"I played at Wembley but four days later was in the reserves. That was devastating," he admitted. "I thought I was playing OK. I didn't do anything startling at Wembley, but I didn't think I'd done anything wrong.

"Even the coaching staff were telling me I was playing well. It was tough to accept being dropped, but I was determined to get back into first grade, just as Jon Scales had done earlier.

"This should act as a warning to the other players. Anything can happen in this game."

Huddersfield had been hovering all season, and were determined to get their man.

"I was on holiday in Florida just before the season started when I first heard of Huddersfield's interest," explained Cook.

"When I got back home I asked Matthew about it and he said he wouldn't let me go. That reassured me but then last week it surfaced again. Matthew still said he wanted me as part of his squad, but Huddersfield had come in with a great offer. He said the directors were keen for the deal to go through, so I talked to Huddersfield earlier this week and made my mind up to sign.

"I had the time of my life at Bradford. They're the biggest club in the game for me, and I'll go to watch them as often as I can. I wish them all the best."

It was a busy 48 hours for the Bulls. Cook departed and Kevin Crouthers arrived from Dewsbury to take his place, but it was quickly back to league action and the game that saw the Bulls equal St Helens' sequence of twelve Super League wins.

But the 42-28 win against Oldham was possibly their most fragile performance of the season. As with the previous fixture at Boundary Park in March, Oldham felt aggrieved that they had nothing to show for their efforts.

The Bulls were still without long term broken limb victims Jeremy Donougher and Sonny Nickle, and they lacked the inventiveness of Robbie Paul, the tireless work of the injured Bernard Dwyer, and, for the first time all season, the driving force of the suspended Graeme Bradley (Bradley was suspended for one match after being put on report for a high tackle late in the Warrington game).

The Bulls accelerated away from the start and charged into a 10-2 lead. The 13,000-plus fans settled back for the expected rout, but the gallant Bears had other ideas. The league leaders stuttered in their attempts to

Paul Loughlin scored a late try at Halifax to secure a
30-26 win after the Bulls had trailed 26-6.

pull away and the Bears took a shock 18-10 lead at the break.

Matthew Elliott disappeared into the tunnel with some tough talking to do.

"They gave us a lesson in enthusiasm and desire. I compliment them for doing everything stronger, faster and better than us in the first half," he said afterwards.

Whatever Elliott said to his players at the break, combined with the noticeable introduction of substitutes Nathan Graham and Paul Anderson, turned the tide, as the Bulls emerged to stun the Bears with a blitz of five tries in 15 minutes.

Next up was a Tuesday night visit to Halifax. Victory would create a record 13 straight Super League victories. For most Bulls supporters, it turned out to be the game of the season. The only pity was that many stayed away, justifiably angry at Halifax's decision to increase admission prices for the game.

The 30-26 win put the Bulls seven points clear, but it took an almighty comeback to rescue a game that appeared beyond them when Halifax held a 26-6 lead at the break thanks to the brilliance of their attack and some relentless defence.

Everyone watched in almost disbelief as Halifax stretched out to 20-0 before Brian McDermott's long reach brought the Bulls first try. With 20 minutes remaining, Halifax seemed content to sit back on their lead, which looked unassailable.

But James Lowes refused to accept defeat and put Simon Knox over with a lovely delayed pass. Paul Loughlin goaled and within minutes Spruce had gone over twice. Scales then powered through a double tackle, and Loughlin's kick hit the post and left it at 26-all

Lowes speculative kick to the corner wasn't dealt with by Damian Munro, and Loughlin just got his hand to the ball to cap a dramatic finish.

"I'm gobsmacked," said an almost speechless Elliott.

He wasn't quite as ecstatic with the Bulls next win, 40-24 at Salford, which was largely thanks to the brilliance of Graeme Bradley.

"I thought Salford played well throughout the match but we played positive rugby in sapping conditions," he said.

Off the field, the Bulls began the build-up to the World Club Championship by launching a new strip. The design was similar to that worn at Wembley when the Bulls were forced into manufacturing a new kit to avoid a colour clash with St Helens.

"We have been inundated with requests for replicas of the Wembley shirt, but that was a one-off and it was never intended to offer that shirt to supporters," said Bulls' marketing manager Peter Deakin.

"But that demand has prompted us to launch this new shirt. It's the same style as our Wembley shirt but retains our normal colour of predominantly white."

The shirt featured exclusive World Club Championship badging, and would be worn throughout both phases of the series.

Deakin also used the kit launch to further promote the three home games against against Auckland, Penrith and Cronulla. Demand had already been massive, with local hotels being used in attractive weekend packages that lured people from far and wide.

Over £50,000 worth of tickets had already been sold, and the club confidently predicted bumper crowds for each game. With thirteen straight wins behind them, the Bulls were confident they would match their fans' expectations.

9
A World Stage

THE World Club Championship was being touted as the biggest, most ambitious club tournament of any sport anywhere in the world, ever.

It was certainly the most adventurous event Rugby League had undertaken, and though the format of including all 22 Super League clubs from both sides of the world was revolutionary, to a handful of players the idea at least was nothing new.

Wigan first took Rugby League's ultimate club prize when they defeated Manly on an emotional night at Central Park in 1987. Two years later Widnes thrashed Laurie Daley's Canberra 30-18 at Old Trafford and, in 1991, Wigan regained the title by beating the Penrith Panthers 21-4 at Anfield.

Playing in the centre for the Panthers that night was a familiar name. Graeme Bradley.

Six years on, he was a key figure in the Bulls' backline and was now determined to destroy the Panthers' hopes of reaching a second World Club Championship final.

"There's only Royce Simmons (now coach) still involved from when I was there, and Steve Carter who played stand-off in that game against Wigan," said Bradley. "It's a long time ago and since then I've been at Castleford for a year and St George after that.

"Our chances of winning the tournament depend on injuries. It's important that we win at least two matches. If we can then get another one or two victories in Australia we should qualify. Ideally we would have a full squad to select from, but we haven't. With a bit of luck we'll get a couple of victories.

"By the end of the season all the teams remaining in the competition will be suffering from the same fatigue factor. It will be like having two competitions in one."

The Bulls, already famed for their superb gameday presentation, lined up a sensational entertainment package for the three-game series. Chart topping band T'Pau performed before the opener against Penrith. At half-time there was a parade of Harley Davidsons, and a competition to win a trip for four to the World Club Championship Final in Australia.

For the Auckland game Stax of Soul were booked, and for the final game against Cronulla, The Commitments flew in specially from Dublin.

Added to this was the usual family-orientated entertainment around the outer bowl such as bouncy castles, face painting, fire eaters, jugglers and stilt walkers. It was all a vital part of building the Bulls brand, and the club placed great emphasis on this part of their operation.

The club had invested heavily during the off-season in a packed summer schedule of pre-match showcases. Gary Tasker worked closely with Dave King of Bradford-based Engine Room Productions. New for the '97 season was a bigger stage with an inflatable surround.

"It's the sort of outfit that you would normally see at a major outdoor concert," explained King. "It has a very sophisticated sound and lighting system that allows for feedback because the shape of Odsal means the music bounces around. With a conventional system it would be very confusing for the musicians because they would hear what they had played or sung a few moments after they had actually done it."

Tasker and King often met for long meetings to plan out gameday entertainment, and took personal pleasure in trying to come up with bigger, better ideas.

"The best yet has been the helicopter we had last season against Halifax," said Tasker. "That was incredible and blew people's minds away."

Another key part of the pre-match entertainment was the Bullettes cheer squad. The Bulls had flirted with cheerleaders with limited success since 1989, but the switch to summer and the unique Bulls experience meant a total revamp. Hazel Robson, a member of the original 1989 cheerleaders and qualified choreographer, recruited a new team of experienced dancers who trained at least twice a week and lifted the image of cheerleading to a whole new level. A wardrobe of colourful costumes and complex dance routines gained them recognition throughout the game, and the RFL hired them to perform before major games at Wembley and Old Trafford. Appearances at local galas and the growing number of Bulls Roadshows added to their popularity and led to the formation of the Junior Bullettes when over 200 girls eager to become a Bullette signed up for tuition. It all helped create the unique bond between club and supporter, as fans of all ages clamoured for a piece of the Bulls.

By the time Penrith arrived at Odsal in June, that special Bulls reputation had spread as far as Australia. Officials from all the visiting clubs were keen to take in the atmosphere at Odsal and learn from the Bulls expertise at presenting a game of Rugby League. Shane Richardson, chief executive of Cronulla Sharks and a key figure in the Super League hierarchy, spoke for all of them.

"What Bradford has done is incredible. No Australian club, even Brisbane Broncos, has managed to create something as special as this. I enjoyed myself more at Odsal than I have done at any game for 20 years. The marketing and promotion is superb and they have set the standard for everyone else to match."

On the field, the Bulls were keen to win the same adulation. It was no exaggeration when the media said they carried the hopes of a nation when they faced the Penrith Panthers.

Royce Simmons, the Panthers coach, knew what to expect from the unbeaten leaders of Euro Super League and was concerned.

"We're struggling a little. Our blokes have been waking up at three o'clock in the morning. I've been trying to get them all to stay awake in the day so they can get into a routine, but there is not much you can do about it.

"I've been watching a lot of the Bulls games on video. They are a very strong team, a big side who offload well, and they have a couple of playmakers on the fringes that can take advantage. Tomlinson, Paul and McNamara are all in tremendous form."

The Bulls were billed as the English side most like an Australian team, but Simmons dismissed the relevance of the comparison.

"I don't know about being Australian type of side, they are just a good side. They do all the little things right. They play the ball quick, they control the ball and finish their sets of six. They've got the basics of the game right."

A couple of days before the game, Steve McNamara had a strange duty to fulfil. He saved the Bulls a postage stamp by dropping the match passes at the Panthers' hotel near his home. It gave him the chance to meet up again with Simmons, his old boss at Hull. More than anyone, McNamara knew what the Panthers' strengths were.

"Royce was always totally focussed and intense as a player, and he has carried that into his coaching. At Hull he engendered a great team spirit. That's never a problem when he is around.

"That seems to be what Royce is building at the Panthers. They are not the flashiest side in the competition, but they make up for that with their team play. Everything they do is at 100 per cent, fiercely intense. We expect a physical game.

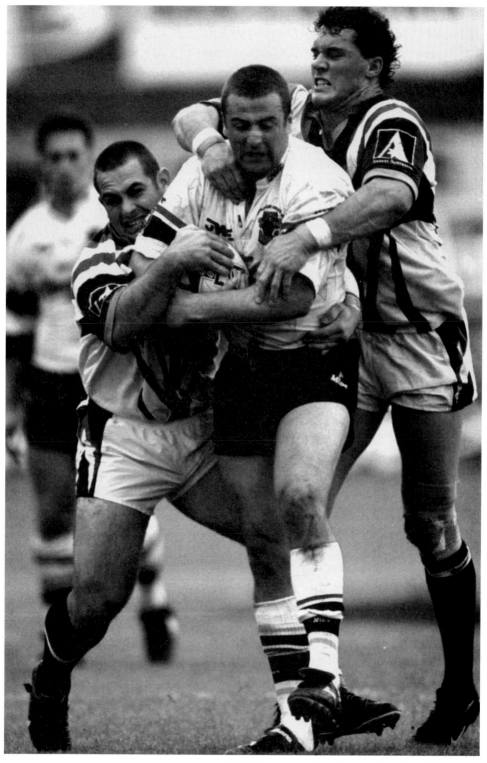

Matt Calland takes the ball up against Penrith Panthers.

"Last week we prepared as though it was another game. The only difference will be that it is harder to put faces to the names that you hear on the videos with a view to picking up individual players on the field."

McNamara was more than looking forward to the game when he arrived at Odsal nearly two hours before kick-off.

"It's the sort of night that you play the game for. In years to come it will be great to look back and recall occasions like this," he said.

Unfortunately, it wasn't quite the night he hoped for. It was a game Bradford Bulls could, and should, have won relatively comfortably. They had the lion's share of possession, put together more creative passages of play and had, by far, the best scoring opportunities. It was an unbearably tense match, but the end result was sheer frustration.

Frustration that the simple final passes went to ground when it mattered. Frustration that British referees seem to have got the message from somewhere that our clubs suddenly have to start playing to Australian interpretations. The play-the-balls frequently bordered on the farcical, and there was a proliferation of high tackles. Referee David Campbell incurred the wrath of the Odsal crowd for his willingness to do nothing more than issue a warning to the first high shot by Panthers captain Steve Carter.

It didn't stop his side re-offending. Four times to be exact, and each time the result was merely a penalty and a ticking off for the guilty party. Understandably, after the match, Bulls' coach Matt Elliott was less than pleased.

"There was one person on the field this evening who is not a full-time Rugby League professional and I thought it showed," he said, clearly trying to retain his usual even temper.

"I'll leave you to decide who that was. If you walk into my dressing shed, have a look at my players' lips and ask them how their necks are."

Carter's crack on Graeme Bradley's chin came just as Bradford's first attack of the evening was clicking into gear. Bradley, at loose-forward to accommodate the returning Robbie Paul, lay in a daze on the Odsal turf for several minutes.

The Panthers' standoff later went on to be one of their most influential players, but he was more than lucky to remain on the field. From the resulting penalty the Bulls surged up-field and registered their first points, a Steve McNamara penalty after Penrith were adjudged offside.

The Bulls time and again tore into the Panthers' defence, and were rewarded when Paul Loughlin neatly put away his winger Jon Scales for a try in the corner. Peter Jorgensen levelled the scores but that only served to spur the Bulls into further action, and Danny Peacock went in off a superb pass from Lowes to push the Bulls out in front again.

Glen Tomlinson kicked through brilliantly for Stuart Spruce to pounce and by the break the Bulls were 16-6 ahead. The game was there for the taking, but the pressure could not be turned into points.

Penrith, looking ever more fast and dangerous on the break were sniffing around picking up the scraps. When Spruce kicked the ball aimlessly in attack, Craig Gower pounced to feed Girdler and the talented centre left the Bradford defence for dead over fifty metres. When Darren Brown went in to level the scores it was as if a giant balloon had been punctured, but the huge crowd found its voice again momentarily to put Girdler off his conversion. They knew that their heroes had thrown it away though, especially when, McNamara inexplicably put wide a field-goal he would normally have back-heeled from right in front of the Penrith crossbar.

It proved costly. The Panthers went straight up the other end and Carter tried for a one-pointer of his own, only to see it charged down by Jeff Wittenberg. The ball squirted out to the lurking Sid Domic who waltzed round the bemused McNamara and Scales.

"It was a game we should have won but we made a couple of errors on our line and Penrith went away for tries at the other end," sighed Elliott.

"I thought we played a positive style of rugby and Penrith struggled to handle us. They didn't build for points as we did, and they had to live off our scraps. We should have cleaned up those scraps but didn't."

Graeme Bradley hadn't received any favours from his former side.

"I got suspended for hitting a bloke on the shoulder so I don't know what's going to happen to those blokes. Steve Carter knocked my head off in the first tackle."

Five days later, the Bulls took the field against Auckland. Incredibly, the result was exactly the same as against Penrith. Once again they went tantalisingly close only to throw it away in the last few minutes.

Somehow, Warriors' rookie winger Paul Staladi found an overlap in the 74th minute to take the Kiwis into a decisive hard-earned lead and kill off any hope Bradford had of making amends for their first night disappointment earlier in the week despite the fact that the Warriors had played the entire second half with only twelve men. Hooker Syd Eru had been sent off just before the break for a high tackle on debutant Andy Hodgson, plucked from the obscurity of local rugby union to make his debut against one of the world's top Rugby League sides.

Auckland skipper Matthew Ridge was in no doubt afterwards as to the importance of the result to the Warriors.

"I've only been at the club for a short time," he said, "but that has to be one of the all-time great wins for the club in its three-year history.

Stuart Spruce looks for support.

"We arrived here as the bottom side in our competition, we were taking on the unbeaten runaway leaders of the British game, and we were doing it with twelve men after thirty minutes or so.

"But we spoke about it at half-time, and made a point of saying that it perhaps could be a turning point in the club's history if we could win this one. Everyone wanted to be part of that."

The game had been set up beforehand as a battle between the two scrum-halves and former team-mates, Robbie Paul and Stacey Jones. It was never really a contest. Paul, struggling to overcome the ankle injury sustained in the Wembley defeat in May, was out of sorts as Auckland raced into an 8-0 lead.

Paul Medley appeared from nowhere to heroically bundle Sean Hoppe into touch, but chances went begging at the other end. The double substitution of Nathan Graham and Paul Anderson seemed to momentarily provide much needed inspiration, but Matt Calland couldn't ground the ball after crossing in the corner.

James Lowes looked as though he'd done the trick, but his pass to the lurking Graeme Bradley was deemed forward. It was that sort of night, especially when Paul Loughlin had the line at his mercy but, instead of holding on to the ball and crashing over for an inevitable try, sent out a shocking pass which landed about a yard behind new boy Hodgson. The chance was gone.

Bradley, back at centre after his brief sojourn at loose-forward, belied the age of his legs and stormed up the right touchline, leaving Tea Ropati and then Denis Betts floundering, for the try the Bulls needed so badly. A superb Steve McNamara touchline conversion brought the scores level, but then Ridge converted his own try to put the Warriors six points in front again.

Forshaw went in under the posts, despite a high tackle from Mark Horo. Loughlin stood in to convert the try and we were all square again. All it needed was another quick score but, as against Penrith, they failed to turn chances into points and, for the second time in a week, they were denied victory in the closing moments.

"We blew it again," admitted Elliott.

"To be honest I thought that in the main we played really appalling, but there is a reason for that. We had Bernard Dwyer playing in the side in the morning, but he had to pull out at the last minute and that was pretty much the story of our side.

"We already had Stuart Spruce out and Robbie Paul, Brian McDermott and Danny Peacock all played busted. You add to that Sonny Nickle, Jeremy Donougher and Warren Jowitt, and when you consider how many players we do have out I feel that we are doing well to compete as we have done, especially against a team of internationals.

"Robbie has struggled with his foot injury, and I perhaps should accept some responsibility for sending him out there when he is not at his best. He went well in training but it was hard for him once the game got going. But I haven't got a lot of people standing out there and putting their hand up for a shirt in those positions at the moment.

"I would have made the same decisions if we had been playing British opposition. I always look to put out the strongest side available. We were putting together a squad that I viewed as a strong one, but the injuries are really testing it to the full. When we were 16-14 ahead we should have closed them down, but we communicated poorly and a pass that was intended for a player went to ground.

"It proved to be a vital play. They scored off that set. We should have kept hold of the football, especially against a side of this quality. We did it against Penrith and I am disappointed that they didn't learn from it. The majority of points are scored in the first and last ten minutes of each half, and if you give the opposition the ball you have to defend. Unfortunately we didn't have enough strength to deal with it.

"Yet I can't afford to be too down in the mouth, because we did compete despite all the injuries that have been working against us. We showed a lot of character and that is really encouraging to give me something to take out of the match."

The two heartbreaking defeats made the Bulls the 'Hard Luck Larrys' of the World Club Championship, but in their hearts the Bulls knew that, as at Wembley, they blew it big style when it really mattered. Their third and final game in the opening rounds gave them an opportunity to rid themselves of that frustration. Standing in their path was the might of Cronulla Sharks.

Graeme Bradley insisted his battered troops could bounce back and take the bite out of the Sharks' fearsome attack.

"We've been vindicated by our performances," he said. "We've lost both games by four points, and each time it was to a last minute try.

"We haven't played as well as we can, but there is nothing between the Bulls and the Australian sides. What people forget is that we've played over 20 games since February. Cronulla have played twelve, and they've had time off when the Tri-Series was on. When they had a midweek competition in Australia everybody screamed blue murder.

"If you subjected the Australians to the same number of games as we have, they too would be fatigued. We are carrying so many injuries. Australia has tailored its competition so there are only ten teams playing one game a week. They can have four sessions a week in the gym, and maintain peak fitness because of that. We had a Challenge Cup semi-final on the Saturday, went to Castleford on the Tuesday, and played London on the Sunday."

Bradley found an ally in Shane Richardson.

"Australian coaches simply wouldn't do it," he agreed. "We have played twelve games and have six to go. Before the next phase of World Club games starting we have three games, whereas Bradford have five plus all the travel.

"Bradford are the team to beat. St Helens may have won at Wembley, but the Bulls have won thirteen on the bounce. They've matched the intensity offered by Penrith and Auckland, and should really have won both those games. That makes Friday's game all the tougher for us."

The Sharks played the Bulls just four days after they had faced St Helens, a point not lost on Bulls prop Brian McDermott.

James Lowes scatters the Auckland defence.

"They might understand how we feel," he joked. "We've had six days to prepare for this, and I almost feel as though I've been on holiday!

After the closeness of the two previous games, the Cronulla game was a big letdown. Mat Rogers, with 26 points, equalled the Sharks' points-scoring record, and every one came as a result of Bulls' errors.

Two of his three converted tries followed slips by desperate Bulls trying to cover a kick through, the other came from an interception. And three of the winger's seven goals were penalties. The Sharks scored only one other try. Though it was a well-worked touchdown by Tiaan Strauss, it came just after Bradley had been dispatched to the sin-bin for dissent in the 29th minute.

Cronulla soaked up all the Bulls threw at them on a wet, misty night and were always in total control. Occasionally they produced flashes of inspirational football, taking full advantage of the rain and slippery conditions to have the Bulls slithering all over the place.

Bradford's play lacked that extra fire which had swept them to the top of Super League. A crop of injuries and a hectic programme of games left them jaded, and in no state to meet Australia's best or even second best.

Significantly, Bernard Dwyer earned the man of the match award after missing six matches through injury.

"It was great to be back, but I am not 100 per cent fit," he said.

"The Aussies certainly play it tough, and their defence is terrific. But we contributed to our own downfall with an interception. Paul Loughlin slipped when he should have had a kick safe, and there was the try that was given by the video ref. That's 18 points off our mistakes, and you can't afford to do that against any side, never mind one as good as Cronulla.

"But we get another crack at them, and I can't wait to get out and play them in Australia."

Sonny Nickle had also returned after a seven-match injury layoff, and celebrated with a last minute try.

Paul Medley halted by tough Auckland defence.

"We played well, but were outclassed by Cronulla," said Paul Loughlin afterwards. "They were too fast, and although we made our own mistakes they were always too good for us.

"But it has been a great experience, and has made us fully aware of just what it means to concentrate for the full 80 minutes, and what you can achieve if you manage to do that.

"It is not easy coming to Bradford, and Cronulla showed their class in playing like it was their home ground. They are a top class side."

Matthew Elliott drew some consolation from the game.

"The coach was out-coached," he smiled. "I'll be a better coach for the experience and hopefully that will help me to make Bradford into a better team.

"It would have been interesting to see what the result would have been if we had been playing anyone else but unfortunately for us we played a Cronulla side bang on top of its game. Having said that, I thought the efforts of my players were outstanding. The score-line wasn't a fair indication of the match. We were a little closer than 30-10."

Not for the first time, Elliott was keen to speak to Greg McCallum, the RFL's Controller of Referees.

"We did let ourselves down a bit with discipline, although I have to say that I need some help in that direction from Greg McCallum. I have to speak to him about some of the decisions that were made. I would probably have been got sin-binned because I was blowing up a bit from my vantage point too, at some of the decisions that were made. They weren't monumental decisions that affected the outcome of the game, but they may have affected our for and against a little bit, and that is important at this stage of the competition."

Elliott also revealed a little ploy he had noticed that perhaps went unnoticed to the untrained eye.

"In Australia they are not obsessed with getting the man straight down to the ground when they make a tackle. They actually hold him up and work and drive him around so that by not laying on him and keeping him upright, they can actually buy time for their defensive line to get back. Even when someone spins through their line a little bit, the tacklers work to hold him up and the defence gets set for the next play. In that way they don't get drawn in and that stops the opposition getting a roll on.

"It has been a real lesson to me and, I am sure, other coaches in England, but everything I have learned is down in my coaching manual now. We will be working on a few things during the week, ready for the Leeds game next weekend. We must concentrate on Super League now, and although we may have lost three on the trot, the teams we play in the next four matches haven't won any games either.

"The only advantage that Leeds will have is that they haven't played a game in two weeks, and we could really have done with such a situation to give us a rest we need. Everyone has come through okay with only Danny Peacock seeming to have suffered a bit of a knee knock.

"Not all of them were 100 per cent fit, but we don't get that chance these days."

10

NO CONTEST

ON the weekend that Mike Tyson and Evander Holyfield entered the ring for the much-hyped 'Judgement Night', another huge battle was predicted at Headingley.

The Bulls were in town and their arch-rivals, the Rhinos, sitting in second place and still harbouring title ambitions themselves despite the seven-point gap, were convinced they could catch the Bulls cold after their long flight back from Australia. With three World Club Championship defeats behind them, the Bulls' unbeaten run looked vulnerable.

Leeds turned up the heat by launching a poster campaign designed to prey upon the jangled nerves of their Challenge Cup semi-final conquerors.

"Iestyn Harris versus Robbie Paul - No Contest" the poster provocatively promised. "Revenge will be sweet. See the Bulls get Bulldozed."

It was the proverbial red rag. Emotions were already simmering after the explosion at the McAlpine Stadium on Easter Saturday, when Bulls prop Brian McDermott had given the Rhinos a boxing lesson, and James Lowes squared up famously with Gary Mercer.

"Leeds win a couple of games and suddenly they fancy their chances, but that's a laugh," blasted a fired up Chris Caisley, who works in Leeds and was keener than most for a Bulls victory.

"They felt aggrieved at losing the semi. It explains their approach to Sunday's game. It's a big game but there will only be one outcome."

Rhinos chief Gary Hetherington was delighted with the campaign and believed he was winning the psychological war.

"Yes, we have been aggressive in promoting this game, and I don't apologise for that," said Hetherington. "It's a very big derby and a very important game. We think we can de-rail Bradford on Sunday. They don't frighten us. In fact they should fear what we can do to them. They still have to play St Helens and London away, and Wigan and ourselves at home. When we win this game they'll be devastated, and it will blow the title race wide open again. We go into the game very confident."

His coach Dean Bell agreed.

"It is the biggest game of the season for us. If we don't win our chances of the title have gone. The preparation has been ideal. If this week at training has been a guide, the players are ready for it. Bradford probably see the game as a chance to put one hand on that Championship trophy. We will stop them."

His opposite number Matthew Elliott banned title-talk in his dressing room.

"There are nine games left and 18 points to go for. It's a vital game along the road to achieving our goal. There's never any shortage of emotion when Bradford play Leeds, and particularly when we are first and second on the ladder. There have been some big games between us over the last twelve months. It makes it easier for me, because I don't need to massage the players psychologically. They know what's at stake, and if they can't prepare themselves for a game like this they're in the wrong place."

There were never any worries the Bulls wouldn't be prepared. Graeme Bradley gave them an early lead, and the Bulls soaked up everything the Rhinos offered. Robbie Paul made a try-saving tackle on Barrie McDermott, and Iestyn Harris's kick to the in-goal was bravely caught by Stuart Spruce and, from the drop-out, McDermott eventually burrowed over.

A couple of penalties put Leeds back further in front, but two long passes spreadeagled the Leeds defence and allowed McNamara the space to dummy and go over in the corner. His touchline conversion emphasised his enormous contribution.

Leeds managed to reduce the deficit to two points at the interval, but after the re-start Bradley stormed through a huge gap in a ragged defensive line and had the presence of mind to hold up the ball until Peacock arrived. Nickle was the last man in support to gleefully go over between the posts. The score lifted the Bulls, and a committed swarming defence ensured that Leeds could not get out of their own half.

Spruce mopped everything up at the back, and the impressive McNamara set off on a mesmerising 70-metre touchline run that allowed Tomlinson to put in Nathan Graham.

The Rhinos hit back again through Mercer and, at 24-16, the game was up for grabs until Bradley went clear again to relieve the pressure and a McNamara penalty on the 70th minute settled any nerves. In the dying

Andy Hodgson continued his rapid Rugby League education
with another fine performance at Leeds.

minutes, the Bulls confirmed their superiority when Graham, Wittenberg and Forshaw combined for Andy Hodgson to gleefully came off his wing to score the final try.

Though Leeds hadn't been able to live up their pre-match predictions, the cheeky poster campaign had worked by drawing the biggest crowd for any Super League game in 1997.

"We knew it wouldn't be easy here," said an exhausted Robbie Paul. "It had so much intensity and stress and I'm so proud to get the win. In fact I'm just so proud to be involved with this Bradford side."

"We copped such harsh criticism after our World Club Championship games," added Steve McNamara. "It was great to shut those critics up. We were desperate to win this one and were better than them on the night."

The crazy fixture programme didn't ease, and within three days the Bulls were trotting out at Odsal again for the visit of Castleford Tigers.

The Tigers were struggling at the foot of the table, but a determined show threatened to steal the Bulls' thunder. In the end, it wasn't enough to deny the champions-elect another two points on their seemingly unstoppable march to the title.

But it took two late strikes from Jon Scales to settle the issue after David Chapman had levelled the scores at 20-20 with only ten minutes left on the clock. The Tigers had matched Bradford in every department until then in a game that often threatened to boil over. When it did, in the second half, it was a case of light the blue touch paper and stand back. The fireworks which greeted the final hooter off the pitch were more than matched by the fireworks on it, an 80th minute melee resulting in giant Castleford prop Dean Sampson being red-carded for fighting when most of the 11,873 crowd were thinking about getting the bus home.

Castleford had scored first and it took until five minutes before half-time for the Bulls to get off the mark. In the second half it was a different story, with Tomlinson collecting his second try and others from Steve McNamara and Nathan Graham putting the Bulls in a seemingly unassailable 20-6 lead.

The Tigers, however, had other ideas and hit back to level it until Scales put his mark on the proceedings with his late double. First the giant winger went in at the corner from Paul Loughlin's pass, and then he pounced for an individual try of his own. McNamara added two superb touchline conversions and a late penalty, and the Bulls breathed a huge sigh of relief.

The next victory, at St Helens, made it 16 out of 16 and few victories could have given them as much pleasure as the one over the reigning champions. From beginning to end the Bulls played like a side in

Mike Forshaw feels the force of the Castleford defence

complete control of their own destiny and nothing Saints could do was going to knock them off their stride.

The Bulls were simply on a different level, treating their large and loyal following to a memorable exhibition of quality attacking and vigorous defence. They were simply too big and too hot for the Saints in a first half which saw them establish a 20-8 lead.

Glen Tomlinson and Steve McNamara tormented the Saints in midfield, whilst Graeme Bradley and Brian McDermott consistently and effectively pounded the Saints line, offloading with ease.

And James Lowes simply did what he does best - everything.

"We knew we were in for a hard game, you always are when you play here," he said. "We came to Knowsley Road with a set plan and we knew that if we played to it we would win.

"The Bradford speccies like to win here and it's another step on the way towards our goal. When the other players play well, I play well. It's a good reflection on the rest of the lads."

It was no surprise when Lowes himself opened the scoring as early as the third minute, escaping Newlove's clutches to dive over from close range.

The Bulls continued to pressurise, but Sean Long romped home from 30 metres to lock the score at 4-4.

Anthony Sullivan raced 90 metres only to be brought back by Mr Cummings for offside and moments later Bulls winger Andy Hodgson rounded off fine work by Tomlinson and McNamara, though the touchdown was too wide out for McNamara to convert.

Matt Calland darted over to extend the lead to 12-4, with McNamara adding an excellent conversion for good measure. Lowes then took maximum advantage of the Bulls' big share of possession to stroll virtually unopposed through a statuesque Saints defence to touch down with ease.

Calland scored his second immediately after the interval following a Sonny Nickle blast with McNamara converting to make the score 26-8. The Bulls had to wait 16 minutes for their next score, but it was well worth the wait. Lowes once more was the chief destroyer, giving Peacock the easiest of chances wide on the right.

Bradley's 65th minute score was simplicity itself, coming from McNamara's perfectly weighted chip and his fifth conversion took Bradford out of sight at 36-8 before Saints grabbed late consolation tries.

On the way out of Knowsley Road, the Bulls passed the Saints boardroom where the gleaming Super League trophy was proudly sitting in a glass cabinet. Metaphorically at least, the Bulls were taking it back across the Pennines with them.

"Bradford are a very powerful side who were too big and too strong for us," said Saints coach Shaun McRae.

"They are a very aggressive team who dominate and intimidate and were too good on the day. I can't speak highly enough of their organisation. They've got a tremendous set up and have improved enormously. No excuses, no complaints, they are going to be worthy winners."

Before jetting off for the second phase of the World Club Championship, the Bulls maintained their winning run by defeating Salford Reds. It confirmed their nine-point lead, and Matthew Elliott brimmed with confidence after a performance which was not the Bulls' most commanding, but achieved the necessary result.

"Salford made one error in the whole of the first half," pointed out the

Bernard Dwyer takes on his old club St Helens

Bulls coach. "They are a team that makes you work hard, and you are not going to force an error unless you are a bit aggressive."

"That X factor was missing in the first 40 minutes, but we kicked up a gear in the second half and it's the sign of a good side when they can just change the personality of the game like that."

"I'm looking to return from Australia and New Zealand with three wins under our belts, and I really think we are capable of doing it. I've got a better squad to choose from in the return matches. Robbie Paul has been running in training like we know Robbie Paul can run, and remember Bernard Dwyer and Sonny Nickle were also missing for most of the first three games.

"A lot of people focussed too much on the results, and not on how well we competed. Those results are like an exposed nerve. I still go 'ouch' when I think about the chances we wasted, but now we have an opportunity to do something about them."

One thing the Bulls couldn't take down under was their fanatical support. Another massive audience again turned out on a sun-drenched summer's evening to cheer their heroes on against Salford. Their contri-

Graeme Bradley makes a break against Salford

bution was again acknowledged by Elliott, and didn't go unnoticed in the opposing dug-out either, where Andy Gregory, justifiably pleased with his side's efforts, paid tribute to the home support and its effect on the outcome.

"In the second half we blew 18 points, and you can't come to Odsal and get away with that," said Gregory. "They've got 14,000 fans and the atmosphere's tremendous - they've really got things buzzing."

The game was a personal triumph for winger Andy Hodgson who raced the length of the pitch to score, a fine reward for an outstanding contribution from the novice who chased and tackled with venom, and mopped up a bombardment from the air.

Elliott beamed with delight at his exploits.

"His hands are magic. A couple of times the ball came at him, and I got half way through shouting 'let it go' when it was in his hands and he was off. He's a natural sportsman. He's a good cricketer, and if you played him at tennis or squash he'd probably beat you at that too!"

While Hodgson looked forward to the trip Down Under, another Bulls winger had to cope with the disappointment of being left at home. Jon Scales had suffered a severe dead leg in the opening game of the World

Club Championship against Penrith, and was still feeling the side effects. He had made an impressive comeback against Castleford but limped out of the Salford game when the pain become to much. His size and power was a vital part of the Bulls' attack, and his absence against the Australasian sides would be a huge blow.

"Jon's had a scan that has revealed serious damage and he's going to be on the sidelines for three or four weeks," revealed physio Karen May. "He's torn a bit of tendon from the bone around the knee cap."

"It is a big big blow because I thought he was showing his best form again after a lean spell," added Elliott. "He's pretty down about it but I've told him there will be other big games around the corner."

Elliott had other problems to deal with before boarding the flight to Auckland. Abi Ekoku had a hand injury and Danny Peacock entered hospital for an operation to remove a piece of floating bone from his wrist.

But something else concerned Elliott. Jeremy Donougher, still out injured after three months, was keen to secure his future. His contract wasn't due to expire until October, but he was concerned at becoming the forgotten man of the Bulls. Added to that, his wife was back in Australia pursuing her business interests.

"We've had initial talks with Jerry and told him we would like him to stay, but it hinges on matters that are more important than rugby," explained Elliott.

"It's a personal thing and something only he can decide. His wife has spent 16 years building up a career in Australia and decided to stay put when Jerry came over to join us. Now they have to decide together what is best for their future."

But there was something that brought a smile to Elliott's face that week. James Lowes, whose influence was growing by the week, agreed an extension to his contract that tied him to Odsal until the turn of the century.

11
Surf's Up!

THE Bulls arrived in Auckland desperate to avenge the heartbreaking 20-16 defeat the Warriors had inflicted on them at Odsal a month earlier, but they were also keen to use the trip Down Under to study the inner-workings of the Australasian clubs and bring back ideas that could be implemented at Odsal to strengthen the Bulls organisation.

Chairman Chris Caisley, director Stephen Coulby and president Colin Tordoff went with the players, while development officers Andy Harland, Steve Fairhurst and Darrall Shelford travelled independently. All were keen to learn as much as possible about training facilities, administration, youth development - anything that could improve the Bulls.

The party were keen observers at the Bulls' first training session in Auckland, an early morning workout on the weights at the Warriors' gymnasium in suburban Penrose.

Their presence brought a smile to Graeme Bradley, who reckoned the venue would provide a rude awakening for the Bulls.

"You could get our gym at Bradford into this gym at least ten times, probably more. The facilities for preparing players in Auckland, compared to Bradford, are just unbelievable. It is a good thing to have our directors out here so they can see the differences with their own eyes.

"It's like sending journalists back to manual typewriters while the newspaper over the road is all on computers, and they are given the same deadline and told to compete with the other lot."

Bradley was looking forward to the game, insisting the pressure would be on Auckland. The motivation for the Bulls, Bradley said, was to shake southern hemisphere fans out of the erroneous belief that Wigan was still Britain's premier team.

"The way this competition is set up it is much more important for the

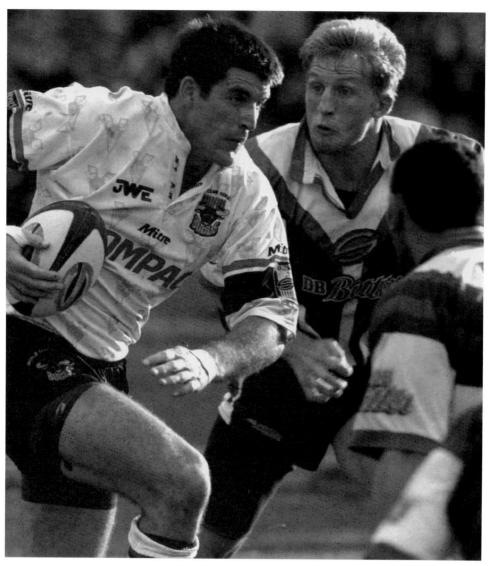

Graeme Bradley charges into the Auckland defence

Australasian teams to win every game than for us," he explained.

"What does it matter if we win two or three games down here? We will qualify for the quarter finals by only winning once. I'll tell you what we think. It is much more important for us to win three games in October than to win six in June and July. Sure, it's a ridiculous way to run a competition but we didn't write the rules. It would be good for English football to win a couple of matches in this round and there's more chance of us doing it than Wigan, I can tell you that.

"We are a far better side than Wigan and to win a game down here would help the Australian public to realise that."

The Bulls had arrived in Auckland to be greeted with a spell of glorious mid-winter weather, and they took full advantage of the sunshine and clear skies on that Tuesday afternoon, preferring an afternoon barbecue at the Waiwera Thermal Pools to another grinding session on the training pitch.

It was just reward. Auckland official Bob Brown, a former Warriors director and father of one-time Salford prop Peter, had been appointed liaison officer to the Bulls and was impressed with their first hit-out, rating the Bulls' effort as the toughest training session he had seen, Australian visitors included.

As the Bulls enjoyed their relaxing afternoon, Matthew Elliott checked on the fitness of Robbie Paul, whose broken thumb was still in plaster.

"It's getting better every day but it's not right yet," Paul told Elliott. "It would be very frustrating to come all this way and sit on the sidelines but I won't play unless I am 100 percent confident of doing the team justice."

Elliott took medical advice and then decided to leave Paul out of his plans.

"I don't want to go against what the experts are telling me, and their advice is that he won't be ready for another week. In any event, we have learned to live without him for much of this season and haven't done too badly!"

Training was gradually stepped up as the week progressed and the players recovered from the long flight. Sessions were held at the famous Carlaw Park ground as well as the huge venue for the game, Ericsson Stadium.

Everything seemed to go well, and Elliott was relaxed and quietly confident when he and Caisley were guests of honour at a special dinner on Friday night, 48 hours ahead of the game.

What happened on the Sunday sent shockwaves throughout the world of Rugby League. The Bulls, unbeaten leaders of the European Super League, were thrashed 64-14 by the bottom club in the Australasian Super League. It had all gone horribly wrong, and no-one could explain why.

"I didn't think for one moment there would be a 50-point spread. Frankly, we're in shock," said Auckland coach Frank Endacott.

If he was in shock then it was hard to think of a description for opposite number Matthew Elliott.

The Bulls competed for the opening quarter, despite being victims of referee Bill Harrigan's unjustified self-confidence, but playmakers Steve McNamara and James Lowes were badly off colour, eventually subbed, and the Bull-machine quickly fell apart.

Graeme Bradley was head and shoulders Bradford's best competitor and he scored early on by stretching a long arm through the tackles of Gene Ngamu, Stacey Jones and Marc Ellis.

But Warriors stand-off Gene Ngamu was in sensational form with the boot and it was largely due to his sharp-shooting that Auckland carried a 24-8 lead to the break, even though they had scored only three tries to two.

The only indication that the most miserable 22 minutes in the Bulls' history was just around the corner had come just short of half-time.

Sean Hoppe started and finished a gem of a try that must have triggered alarm bells. The Kiwi Test winger bust straight through Lowes' tackle, just in front of his own posts, and scorched to halfway before finding plenty of support.

Half-time seemed to boost Auckland's confidence as much as it drained Bradford's. The Bulls looked strangely lethargic and disorganised as Auckland laid on six tries in 22 minutes to turn a victory into a massacre. Their fleet-footed backs got the home crowd roaring and the rampaging running of prop Joe Vagana and the slick ball distribution of second-rower Kearney completed the damage.

In the wake of the hiding, Bradley recalled a similar day on St George's way to the 1992 Winfield Cup Grand Final.

"A few years ago St George were beaten 61-0 by Manly and turned around and beat Penrith the following week," Bradley told the post-match press conference. "One thing we didn't do then was watch the video," Bradley drawled as he set about the demolition of a rather large muffin.

Elliot wasn't looking for sympathy or excuses.

"It's a bit of a unique experience for us," Elliot admitted. "I'm not elated about it, I can tell you that. That day Graeme was talking about, St George met a Manly team that weren't just red-hot, they were white hot. We came up against an Auckland team in similar mood today.

"I do feel we let ourselves down. Our strengths turned into our weaknesses."

Elliot was referring, in particular, to dreadful ball control that saw the Bulls doing so much tackling that they were almost out on their feet by half-time. He refused to blame jet-lag, saying his team had acclimatised well and prepared thoroughly for the game.

"I fully expected to win today but I know how these players react to adversity. They have been hurt but they will bounce back."

Elliott and Bradley found an ally for their confidence in Warriors skipper Stephen Kearney.

"I was very, very surprised with how we won," Kearney said. "Two days out from the game I was really nervous. Bradford are a much better team than they showed here today. I think they will go to Australia and cause an upset. I think they will turn it around over there."

The Bulls quickly got out of Auckland. For the remainder of the trip they would be based at the beachfront Rydges Hotel at Cronulla, about 45 minutes south of Sydney.

Arriving at the hotel, the players were hurt and upset at the Auckland debacle.

"It was frightening," admitted Elliott, "but rather than investigating why it happened we just need to make sure it doesn't happen again. We had a good analysis of the game. I normally splice the tapes up a bit, but they needed to see the whole of this one, the second half in particular.

"It has been a tough couple of days but now we need to turn it into a positive. I regard it as a wake-up call for myself, and I'm working extra hard to put things right for Monday's game at Penrith."

Steve McNamara vowed they would bounce back and come away from Australia with at least one win.

"It was a relief to get out of Auckland after the pounding we took there. I can't explain what went wrong other than everyone seemed to have an off-day. Hopefully it was one of those freak results that won't happen again for a long time.

"What matters now is that we get ourselves prepared for the Penrith game. It's probably the most important game of the season for us now if we are serious about progressing in this competition."

McNamara was struggling to make the run-out side for the Monday night game, having sustained a calf injury in Auckland.

"I'm having treatment twice daily and I'm desperate to play, but I won't play unless I'm 100% fit. I thought I was OK for the Auckland game but realised after the first tackle that I was going to struggle.

"It sounds silly after the result last weekend, but I really think we can win our games against Penrith and Cronulla. There is no way the Auckland result gave a true reflection of what kind of side Bradford are. We are capable of so much more, as we have shown at Odsal all season.

"I think we have got it out of our system now. We have an eight day break between the games and everyone is already chomping at the bit wanting to put the record straight. We are determined to win at least one if not two of the games over here."

McNamara, no stranger to Cronulla after living there in 1993 whilst enjoying a stint with St George, was left behind at the team hotel for treatment as the rest of the squad took a couple of days off.

"Some of the boys have gone up to Queensland for a couple of days and Jimmy Lowes has gone to Newcastle to see the local team he played for a couple of years ago," he sighed.

"But I'm staying here to make sure I get my injury treated and make the team next Monday."

When the squad reported back for training on Thursday morning, the mood had changed. Once again, the players were switched on and totally focussed on beating Penrith. Two days of rest and relaxation on the sand and surf had recharged their batteries, but one player was still feeling frustrated.

Robbie Paul was having a bad time. A groin injury, followed by a serious thumb injury, had kept him out of the Bulls' lineup for much of the season, and he hadn't recovered in time to play in Auckland, his home territory.

"To put it bluntly I was pissed off at not being able to play in Auckland," said Paul, with disarming frankness.

"It's frustrating watching your mates play. On this occasion I was watching my mates playing against my other mates, back from my days at home, who I would have loved to have played against."

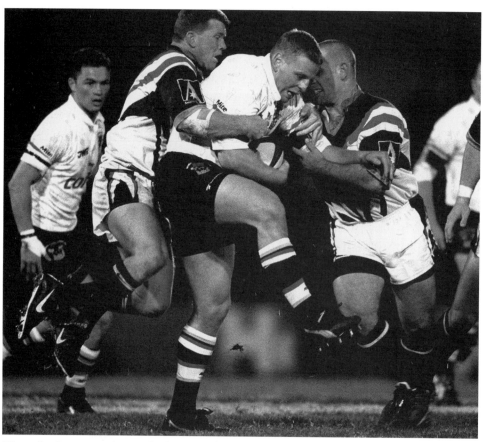

Warren Jowitt never took a step backward at Penrith

Paul gave himself more than fair chance of being named in the Bulls' side to play Penrith.

"I'm burning from the inside. If I'm chosen for selection I'll be thrilled. No one is certain until the coach puts the names on paper. I may have a problem with fitness over 80 minutes, but at least I'm in training, and I would love to be there.

"It's a strange game, this game of ours. It's a huge part of your emotional psyche. If you're not playing you become depressed internally. But when you get out here, and you're able to run about in training, it's such a relief after the inactivity at home. This is midwinter, and yet it's equivalent to summer in England. This is just a good place to be, with a beautiful hotel on the beach. We now have an official Bradford Bulls surf club. We are not very good, but we are having a tremendous time in the surf."

Paul was confident his Bulls could defeat the Panthers.

"We aren't the favourites, but we like going into games as the underdogs. We enjoy that. It takes the pressure off us, so that we can do what we do best.

"We haven't played as badly as we did against Auckland for as long as I can remember. The game surprised everyone. But it was probably good for us in the long run, in bringing us down to earth."

Unfortunately for the Bulls, the Panthers also brought them down to earth with another stunning defeat, this time 54-14.

The Bulls went into the game without McNamara, whose daily treatment hadn't provided the miracle cure. Mike Forshaw stepped up off the bench to take his place, and Paul returned to allow Bradley to revert to the centre.

Two things contributed to the Bulls' downfall. The most important, from the viewpoint of the 100 or more Bulls supporters who had made the trip around the world to follow their heroes, was referee Bill Harrigan's erratic performance, aided by a video referee who seemingly couldn't recognise a try when he saw one.

A penalty count of 15-4 against the Bulls was the telling statistic, and there were several incidents where Penrith got the rub of the green, as coach Royce Simmons admitted afterwards.

The whiff of conspiracy theory was in the air among the Bulls fans in the luxurious Panthers Leagues Club after the game.

"It's not our fault your perm's grown out," shouted one Bradford fan at the hirsute Harrigan.

But the real issue confronting the Bulls was not Harrigan, questionable as his performance was. What really let them down was their own indiscipline. They allowed themselves to get rattled.

Just before the interval James Lowes took a swing at Penrith halfback Craig Gower just ten metres short of the line. With Lowes on his way to the sin bin Gower scored a try, and Bulls centre Matt Calland, claiming to be obstructed in attempting to make a tackle, showed dissent and also received his penance of ten minutes. The Bulls were down to eleven men.

A disallowed try was the other main talking point. Down 10-6, and with Brian McDermott having dropped a gilt-edged chance to put the Bulls in front, Lowes kicked to the corner and Danny Peacock pounced to score what looked a good try. The video ref' thought otherwise, as, surprisingly, did Bulls coach Matthew Elliott.

"It was unlucky, but if I had been the referee I wouldn't have allowed it," said Elliott, to the surprise of the assembled press after the game.

At that stage Mike Forshaw had already scored a superbly created try for Bradford, and another score would have given them the lead.

"I was disappointed not only for our players, but for the fans who travelled around the world to support us, and also for Penrith, who didn't get a chance to play under pressure," said Elliott.

"We were up for this game, but we got nothing from the referee. I don't

Glen Tomlinson cuts through the Cronulla ranks

Matt Calland gets 10 minutes in the bin at Penrith. The Bulls were less than impressed with referee Bill Harrigan

have a problem with Bill Harrigan, but perhaps he has a problem with us. We have a couple of guys who are prepared to ask questions, but they don't deserve that reaction."

One good thing to come out of the game for the Bulls was Robbie Paul's return without any aggravated injury. Paul had a relatively quiet game, but did enough to suggest that he could soon return to form.

It was Paul who fed Peacock ten metres from the line for Bradford's second try after 58 minutes, although by then it was much too late.

Two defeats down, the Bulls had just one more chance of winning a game on Australian soil. Their final opponents would be the most formidable of the three, Cronulla Sharks. Despite the two heavy losses,

Stuart Spruce weaves his way through the Penrith defence.

Warren Jowitt, back in fine form after recovering from his broken ankle, was convinced the Bulls could come good.

"The games over here haven't been what I expected," he said. "Even though we have lost badly they haven't been as fast as I thought. Monday's game against Penrith was just like playing Wigan or Leeds. One man spoilt it as a true contest, and it could have been a totally different game.

"We know we could have won. If the try had been allowed when we were only four points behind Jimmy and Matt would have kept their cool and not gone to the sin bin. We could have easily gone in two points ahead instead of 22-4 down.

"Given a fair chance, I really believe we can beat Cronulla."

Jowitt was one of the Bulls players to benefit most from the exposure of playing against top Australian sides.

"I've learnt a lot just from watching what other teams and players do," he said. "There is much more emphasis on defence here and I've picked up a couple of things that should help my game."

Jowitt's optimism at beating Cronulla was shortlived. The Sharks came out on top by 40-12 as the Bulls ended the group games with six defeats out of six. Amazingly though, they finished third in the European Pool and qualified for the quarter-finals. Penrith, who had won all six games, didn't qualify!

Robbie Paul continued his horror run with injuries, leaving the field with a shoulder injury.

"The injury is rotating round his body," said frustrated coach Matthew Elliott afterwards.

The Sharks tore into the Bulls with determination, allied to the extraordinary flair that has been their trademark. They scored four tries in the first half and, had it not been for a Bulls revival in the first quarter of the second period, the margin could have been much greater than the 28 it eventually was. No-one could accuse the Bulls of playing without pride and commitment, but mistakes were punished mercilessly by the Sharks.

"The main difference between the sides is pace," reasoned Elliott. "Physically our players could compete if you took them into the gym. But they have so much more speed across the park than us."

The Bulls took the field without the injured James Lowes and Andy Hodgson, and the suspended Sonny Nickle, although they welcomed back Steve McNamara at loose forward and Jeremy Donougher for his first game since the start of the Super League season.

Cronulla took the lead after only three minutes in their first serious attack on the Bradford line, and added other tries at an even pace, and the half-time score of 24-0 looked ominous for the Bulls. But they had battled away and created some enterprising attacks before breaking down under pressure.

As the second half got underway the Sharks made a long break from deep inside their own half, with Adam Dykes being put in the clear. Amazingly, Jowitt set off in pursuit and ran him down. That seemed to give the Bulls an injection of confidence and for 20 minutes they took control of the game. Bradley brought them back into it, with two tries as he completely fooled the Sharks defence. For the first one he received the ball 15 metres from the line, and the defence stood off, expecting him to create play for one of his supporting players on either side. But Bradley headed straight for the posts as Sharks defenders watched seemingly with open mouths.

His second effort, scored from a similar position, saw him beating Craig Greenhill and Tawera Nikau. With McNamara adding both conversions the Bulls could suddenly see a chink of light at 12-24.

But then the Sharks asserted themselves once more, and stepped up a gear to pull clear towards the end.

Tahi Reihana, who had played for Perth Reds in the Australian competition, was in reflective mood back at the hotel after the game.

"Both legs of the tournament have been a good experience in exposing us to quality players. Everyone is saying that it's a yardstick against which we can measure our own progress. In that sense I was quite happy with my own form. I'm used to the conditions in Australia, so I suppose that was an advantage.

"To come out here and gain this experience will ensure that we will come back a better side. That is especially so for a player like Warren Jowitt. Warren will be sitting down now thinking that he can mix it with these guys.

"Tonight we were exposed to three State of Origin back-rowers, and we did well against them. The characteristic of their play is to recover in defence when we make breaks. They scramble so well. Maintaining our control of the ball, and sustaining that pressure is what we must learn to do.

"We have learned a little more, and we'll feel stronger going back to play against Leeds next week. We are already focussed on that game. It's a big game for both clubs. We are looking forward to it, and we expect a strong performance in front of our own crowd."

Reihana was keen to pay tribute to the spirit within the Bulls camp.

"This is the most unusual team I've ever been involved with, in that there is no segregation, no cliques, and the boys are all as one. With more time together this side could mature into a team that can compete with anyone."

12

PRIZE BULLS

WITH a crunch game against local rivals Leeds Rhinos awaiting on their return from Australia, the Bulls were looking forward to a quiet, relaxing flight home before going straight back into training.

Instead, the weather conspired against them and they endured a nightmare 45-hour journey after their plane was twice diverted with unscheduled stops in Japan and Hong Kong due to violent thunderstorms.

Nonetheless, the weary Bulls prepared for the game knowing that, if other results went for them, victory could clinch the Super League title.

"I hope Castleford can do themselves and us a big favour with a win against London," said Graeme Bradley," but realistically all we will be concentrating on doing is ensuring that we pick up the league points against Leeds. Anything else is a bonus."

Despite a 5-0 win record over the Rhinos during the previous two years, the Bulls were treating Leeds with the utmost respect.

"They are in second position, have enjoyed some great wins this season to put them there and have to be respected as a side capable of beating anyone on their day," said Bradley.

"There is no doubt that they will be fired up for this one, but so will we. We are disappointed that we didn't win any of our matches overseas, but we are not down.

"We were dreadful against Auckland, had everything go against us in the Penrith game, and were close enough to Cronulla at 24-12 to have won the match, only for it to slip away. But we were able to go home with quite a few positives from that game, in so much as we welcomed back Robbie Paul and Jeremy Donougher and they both had big games. And we achieved our goal and qualified for the quarter-final stages by finishing third in the European group.

"If we win three games against Australasian Super League teams in October, we will be World Champions."

Leeds were hoping to catch the Bulls cold after the arduous journey, and Rhinos winger Francis Cummins stirred things up in the days leading up to the game.

"Bradford have done a superb job both on the playing and marketing side, but we know that if we had a winning team no-one would be able to match us," he boasted.

"There's nothing better than a really big game and they don't come any bigger than this. We know what it was like flying back to face them after phase one of the World Club Challenge and it will be tough for them. Mentally it's not easy to get rid of the travel but they like us won't need motivating.

"We have a huge incentive, they hurt us badly two years running in the Cup and effectively ended any hopes we had for the title this time. The crowd and the atmosphere will be tremendous and all the players will respond to that."

It was the Bulls players who responded the better, securing a 22-8 win that put one hand firmly on the Championship trophy. They extended the record opening run to 18 successive wins, and needed just one more point to bring the major title back to Bradford for the first time since 1981.

The Bulls owed their 14-2 interval lead mainly to the brilliant return to form of Robbie Paul, but the injuries that had dogged him all season continued and he lasted only five minutes of the second half with a shoulder problem.

But for 40 delightful minutes it was the old Paul back to something like his magical best as he scored two tries and created the other. The first of his tries was a truly magnificent effort that even Leeds fans must have grudgingly appreciated. There was nothing on when he took the ball 40 metres out until a quick dummy and a little shimmy left Leeds stranded and Paul scampered away like a cheeky schoolboy.

His second try followed McNamara's short kick through with Paul alert enough to win the dash to touch down for a try awarded after a long video check.

Paul was on the way to walking off with the individual match honours until his injury. Then it was James Lowes who took the eye with a typically grafting performance highlighted by a short-range solo try, not long before he too retired hurt. It was an eventful night for Lowes, who spent a spell in the sin bin after trading blows with his opposite number Wayne Collins.

The Bulls had set the tempo from the very beginning when they

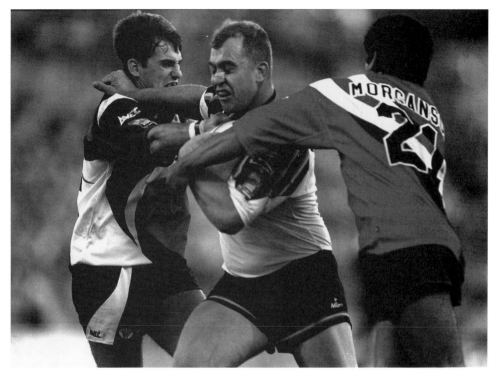

Jeff Wittenberg powers his way forward at Sheffield Eagles

regained the ball from their own short kick-off to put Leeds under immediate pressure. The Rhinos weathered that early blast but cracked after only eleven minutes when Jon Scales went in at the corner off Paul's well-timed pass. It was a reassuring success for Paul who a few minutes earlier had sent a dreadful pass into touch.

Harris pulled back two points for Leeds with a 40-metre penalty goal before Paul struck with the first of his two tries. The 14-2 interval lead was no more than they deserved after completely dominating the game in every department.

Leeds needed an early second-half try to get back into the game and they got it when Marvin Golden twisted and turned to go over off Terry Newton's pass. Iestyn Harris's kick from wide out hit a post but he popped over a simple penalty goal after a few minutes to leave Leeds just six points behind. Paul Sterling almost narrowed the gap further when he snapped up a loose ball and shot for the line only to be hurled into the corner flag by Jeremy Donougher's desperate tackle.

It was virtually Leeds' last fling as Bradford powered back and Lowes went in for his try, slipping through from a play-the-ball 10 metres out on the hour. McNamara tagged on the goal and a 67th minute penalty as Leeds began to become rattled.

Gary Mercer was the major culprit and was put on report for a high, late tackle on Graeme Bradley. Mercer was subsequently banned for the rest of the season.

The win meant that just one point was needed form the next game, away at Sheffield Eagles. The trip to Don Valley was touted as the most significant day in the history of the Bradford club. The day the Bulls could win their first major trophy.

Sheffield Eagles wouldn't roll over, however. The previous week they had conquered Wigan and were hardly likely to lie down and die in the face of the marauding Bulls army.

During the build-up, the Bulls took time out from their gruelling schedule to have a little fun and organised a refuelling session at the local go-kart track.

"Matthew surprised us by bringing the whole squad here for some relaxation," explained Mike Forshaw. "It's the kind of thing that helps ease the pressure.

"I can't wait for the game at Sheffield. I didn't enjoy my time at Saracens and as soon as Bradford said they were interested I couldn't get to Odsal quick enough. I could see what was happening here, and I wanted to be part of it. I knew they were emerging as a real force and hopefully at Sheffield we will confirm that.

Forshaw was on the brink of adding to the three Championship medals he collected at Wigan.

"I remember John Monie saying that the league title is the only thing worth winning. It means you are the most consistent side over the whole season. When I was at Wigan it became such an annual thing that it was almost expected, but this will be Bradford's first for a long time. We are all proud to be in the team that has brought success back to those terrific Bradford fans.

"Being under pressure brings the best out of us. Last Sunday Leeds said they weren't under any pressure, and that it was all on us, but we thrive on it. The title is almost ours, and our next target is to go unbeaten.

"That adds to the pressure, because each team we play now wants to be the first to beat us. If anything that makes us all the more determined. After I'd played four or five games here I sensed that we could perhaps go unbeaten. My old mates at Wigan were saying to me months ago that we couldn't be caught. We are allowing ourselves to talk about it now, although we have some tough games coming up. Wigan and London will be huge games for us, and they will be desperate to upset us.

"But we want to win every game we play, and our next target is the Premiership. That would give us a good platform to go to Auckland and turn them over. They won't have played for five weeks, whereas we have

The back-room staff get to work on bruised Bulls trio Stuart Spruce, Mike Forshaw and Robbie Paul after the World Club Championship defeat at Cronulla

The team hotel for the World Club Championship games in Australia overlooked Cronulla beach, and the Bulls soon formed their own surf club! Matt Calland and Brian McDermott (BELOW) were first to the waves.

(ABOVE LEFT) Stuart Spruce offloads against Cronulla.
(ABOVE RIGHT) Graeme Bradley stopped by his old club
Penrith Panthers.
(BELOW LEFT) James Lowes struggles for extra ground
despite three Auckland defenders.
(BELOW) Robbie Paul skips past Auckland's Mark Horo.

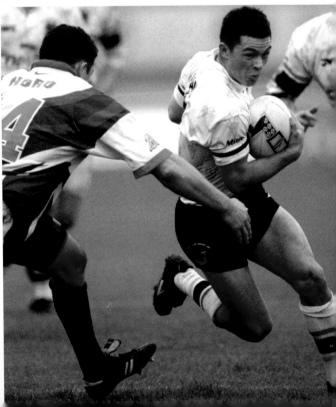

(ABOVE LEFT) Powerful winger Jon Scales capped another solid season with a call-up to the Great Britain squad.

(ABOVE) Simon Knox illustrated his value to the Bulls with five tries.

(LEFT) Andy Hodgson produced a string of superb displays on the wing after being plucked from local rugby union, but his season ended in tragedy with a badly broken leg.

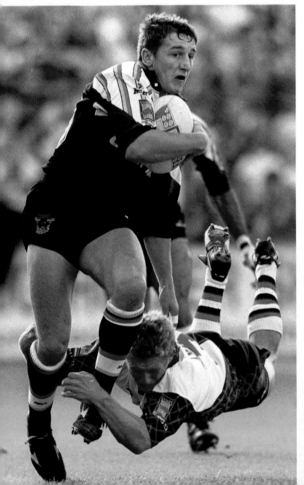

(ABOVE) Tahi Reihana powers through the Sheffield ranks on the day the Bulls wrapped up the title at Don Valley.

(ABOVE RIGHT) Paul Medley at his explosive best in the searing heat at Salford in June.

(RIGHT) Paul Loughlin, who was to end the season on the transfer list, in action at Sheffield.

(LEFT) Giant Australian prop Jeff Wittenberg was a late arrival at Odsal after Michael Hogue made way on the quota by joining Paris St Germain.

Celebration time as the Stones Super League
Championship finally arrives at Odsal.
(CLOCKWISE) The Hookers Union - James Lowes
and Brian Noble; head coach Matthew Elliott;
skipper Robbie Paul.

The champagne began to flow at Don Valley (ABOVE) but there was plenty left for Odsal a week later (BELOW)

Matthew Elliott with daughters Clare, Mia and Lucy and his 'other team' - the Bullettes.

(RIGHT) Five Bulls were selected in the Stones Dream Team - Mike Forshaw, James Lowes, Graeme Bradley, Danny Peacock and Stuart Spruce.

(BELOW) At the glittering end-of-season Stones Man of Steel dinner in Manchester, the Bulls picked up more awards. Matthew Elliott was voted Coach of the Year, and James Lowes scooped a double - Stones Super League Player of the Year and the coveted Man of Steel, the highest individual honour in the game.

learned a lot from our games down there."

Forshaw's form was one of the highlights of the season.

"I'm 26, and I think I'm playing better than ever. I don't see why I can't make the Great Britain squad. And if we bring in a couple of top players we can challenge for honours again next year and build our crowds up even more."

Unfortunately for Forshaw, his form on the race track was the direct opposite of that on the field.

"Bernard Dwyer, Glen Tomlinson and Matthew are the Michael Schumachers," he laughed. "Abi, Sprogger (Stuart Spruce) and I are the ones who spin off on the first corner.

"Tommo and Matty have a score to settle from last time. Tommo was leading all the way until Matty cut him on the last lap. They're having a real dogfight!

"I'm timid. I once saw Graham Holroyd spin and turn over. The kart landed on top of him and it could have been nasty. My excuse is that I have to drive along the M62 every day - now that is frightening!"

The Eagles also took to a race track to relax before the game, and their loose forward Martin Wood was confident of ending the Bulls' long winning run.

"If we can beat Wigan, we can beat anyone," he said defiantly. "Bradford are such a well balanced side. They're massive in the forwards, and Robbie Paul is dynamite. Glen Tomlinson's a good halfback, and Stuart Spruce clears the line superbly from fullback. It could be as close as the Wigan game."

As Saturday dawned, the whole city of Bradford seemed to be caught up with Bullmania. Good luck posters, flags and scarves dangled from house and shop windows, lampposts and cars. The M1 became a convoy of red, amber and black as Bulls supporters set off for the much antici-pated victory that would signal the biggest party the city had ever seen. They came in their thousands - mums, dads, grannies and grandads, young and old - pouring down the motorway in support of the Bulls, bedecked in replica shirts, waving flags and scarves to provide a perfect backdrop to what was an unforgettable sporting experience on a perfect summer's evening.

And Sheffield, on and off the pitch, put on a show. The pre-match entertainment was slick and professional, the PA superb, and the choice of music fitted the mood. It was perfect. It was a night when Don Valley, so often labelled a soulless white elephant, came alive.

For 20 minutes the Eagles, building on their fine victory over Wigan, provided a stern test of the Bulls' title aspirations. It was only when Jeff Wittenberg scored that the Bulls support could begin to breathe easily

The coaching staff celebrate clinching the title at Don Valley. (FROM LEFT) Michael Potter, Brian Noble, Matthew Elliott, Carl Jennings, Darrall Shelford and Karen May.

and begin the party.

Two further Bradford tries in the closing stages to complete a deluge of 18 points in the last nine minutes, made the final scoreline totally unreflective of a tight and compelling encounter. Sheffield captain Paul Broadbent, magnificent in the home pack, was quick to pay tribute to Bradford after the game, and place their achievement into perspective.

"A few years ago, Odsal was a cold, unwelcoming place, with no atmosphere and crowds of a few thousand," he said. "Now the place has come alive, it's an intimidating place to go, and every game is an occasion.

"They say that Don Valley is no good for Rugby League. But it was a great setting tonight, with all those people in, the colour and the noise and the great atmosphere.

"Bradford have shown what can be achieved with great marketing on the back of a successful team. They've turned a real dead hole completely around, and at Sheffield we've got to set out to do what they've done."

And Broadbent's analysis of the Bulls team was spot on: "They've so much quality throughout the side, with one or two really outstanding individuals. They are worthy Champions," he said.

"You look at past Champions, and often they have won quite a few games by very tight margins, just sneaked through. But Bradford, over the course of the season, have won virtually every game on merit."

In the first half Sheffield put in a near faultless performance, and could have been more than six points ahead at the interval. Broadbent and Danny McAllister led a great forward effort, Mark Aston's kicking game was pinpoint in its accuracy, and the backs, with Fijian Waisale Sovatabua revelling in the heat, a constant danger.

The Bulls scored first, as Glen Tomlinson and Steve McNamara quickly moved the ball right and Danny Peacock twisted his way through three attempted tackles. But after Sovatabua had a try ruled out by the video referee for losing control of the ball over the line, the Eagles enjoyed a purple patch and took a 10-4 lead.

The Bulls were flat, their kicking game below standard, their attacks lacking spark.

"In the first half we knew we'd been poor," admitted Steve McNamara afterwards. "It was a real tough game, and the small pitch made it difficult for us. We knew we had to come out for the second half and perform. On the day, the result was the most important thing."

The Bulls' response was almost immediate, the try so typical of many in this title-winning season. Brian McDermott sucked in three or four defenders with a bullocking run which was halted just short. James Lowes, dummying a long ball from the ruck, sent Dwyer over untouched with a delicious, delayed short pass. McNamara's conversion levelled the scores.

But still Sheffield refused to buckle. Their defence held firm as Graeme Bradley tried to squeeze through after a dazzling 50-metre run by Peacock. Then McNamara just failed to get over in a two-man tackle after another superb Lowes break, the try ruled out by the video referee.

When Broadbent broke the siege with another surging run, Spruce was sin-binned for holding down. Aston booted the 19-metre penalty for a 12-10 lead on 52 minutes before the nerveless McNamara got Bradford back in front with two penalties in two minutes.

The intensity of the game, and the boiling sun, led to errors by both sides, and the next try always looked like being the winner. It finally came nine minutes from the end, with Wittenberg bursting through two tired tackles from McDermott's pass for the gamebreaker.

The tension subsided and the celebrations began. Sovatabua halted Peacock's 60-metre run with a magnificent cover tackle, but Tomlinson sent Lowes in amid a crescendo of noise. In the last minute Tomlinson's astute cross-kick eluded Scales, but fell kindly for Mike Forshaw to complete the scoring.

The frowning face of Matthew Elliott, previously chewing gum with concentration, was shown on the big screen. As if on cue, Elliott broke into a massive grin, bringing the biggest cheer of the evening.

It was a superb game, and the crowd, estimated at 10,500 (the exact figure is apparently never provided at this council-owned venue) made it a night to remember.

"This is simply awesome," said Paul after being chaired off the pitch by jubilant fans. "This is what we have been waiting for and wanted for so long. Now with the title in the bag we can go on and win even more."

The Bulls supporters refused to let their heroes go, and constant chanting and singing persuaded the players to return to a specially erected stage in front of the main stand. One by one the players took the applause before James Lowes and Graeme Bradley picked up a microphone to thank them all before the army of fans finally headed towards Bradford for a celebration drink.

Back in the dressing room Brian McDermott unwittingly revealed some of the secrets behind the Bulls' success.

"I made a couple of mistakes out there in the second half," he confided. "I hold my hands up, you can't hide. We'll be looking at the video tomorrow, and that doesn't tell lies. I'll have to make sure it doesn't happen again."

McDermott's words went largely ignored amid the euphoria. But they spoke volumes for the standards Bradford had set. In a compelling struggle, McDermott had been magnificent, his driving runs and workrate an inspiration for his team-mates.

"Everyone at the club's a perfectionist," he continued. "There's no escape.

"I'm chuffed for myself, no doubt, but I'm really pleased for Matthew. He's given so much to this club, as assistant to Brian Smith, and as a coach in his own right. He's got us to Wembley, and he's got us each a Championship medal. And I'm sure we'll go on and achieve more.

"I was a big rawboned lad, eager for work. Matthew helped channel me in the right direction, and knocked off the rough edges. He worked hard on my tackling technique, on developing my skills and cutting down the errors. But most of all he taught me, and all the team, that you can have all the talent in the world, but it's no good if you don't have a go.

"This year, at Bradford Bulls, we had a go."

McDermott was then showered with champagne as he joined the rest of his team-mates.

Elliott went round every player individually, shaking their hands, congratulating and thanking them.

The directors wandered in to join the celebrations, not caring when their expensive suits quickly becoming drenched with the gallons of beer and champagne.

Chris Caisley was keen to pay tribute to the magnificent Bulls support.

"No other sport or club in this country has the type of supporters we have. They were absolutely unbelievable tonight, as they have been all season. We always set out to make them partners in our success. They have a massive part to play and without them we wouldn't be champions."

Caisley also had a special word for coach Elliott.

"When we appointed him we knew his character, his integrity, and his honesty. He had learnt his trade and I don't think it was the gamble many people made it out to be.

"One thing I knew was that if he did fail it wouldn't be through lack of effort. He has put in a

James Lowes and Paul Loughlin
celebrate at Don Valley

tremendous amount of hard work and chose his backroom team very wisely. It brings me back to one thing - teamwork. So many people have played their part in winning this Championship."

Eventually, the players escaped the fans and media and made their way to the VIP lounge to be greeted by more hugs and kisses, this time from wives and girlfriends. Two hours after the game had ended, the Bulls team bus arrived back at Odsal to be met by hundreds of supporters outside the Top House pub. The place was effectively drunk dry before the party moved on to the wine bars and clubs in the city centre.

The following day, Elliott reflected on the amazing scenes at Don Valley, and the Championship-winning season.

"To look around the stadium and see so many Bulls supporters was a humbling experience for me. The team wish to devote that win, and the Championship, to the Bradford spectators. Their backing this season has been magnificent, and has made such a great contribution to our success.

Matthew Elliott is mobbed by hundreds of fans on the pitch at Don Valley

It's been a real team effort, on and off the field, and we've all been in it together.

"After Wembley, we copped the defeat, took it on the chin, and learned from the game. It made us stronger in our resolve to win the Super League title. But the players, and myself as coach, are accountable to so many people, and at half-time we realised we were in danger of letting so many people down.

"It was a really tough game, and I must pay due credit to Sheffield. They put in a fantastic effort and harassed us all evening. The scoreline flattered us, and the 20-point margin was really tough on the Eagles. I may sit there with a stony face sometimes, but I've really enjoyed the season and being part of something so special. At the end of the game the tension just fell away, and we could start to celebrate.

"You look for the reasons for our Championship season. There are so many, too many really to analyse. It's just a special set of circumstances, and things coming together. At Bradford, we have so many good things going for us - the magnificent support, the backroom staff, the coaching team. Most important of all, we have a special group of players with character, a burning will to achieve, and an inability to accept anything less than the best. We had a squad of about 26 players of Super League standard. I can only pick 17 for any one game, so at any time that's nine people disappointed and itching for their chance in the next game. It keeps people on their toes, and makes them perform.

"Look at Mike Forshaw, for example. He came to the club at at a crucial time and became an important member of the team. He got caught up in the atmosphere and went on to new heights as a player. He didn't know he was that good. We had our key players, people like Graeme Bradley and James Lowes, who we couldn't have done without. But overall, it was a team effort. After all, we haven't yet had one man win the player of the month award.

"We did it together. We had a single purpose, and we achieved. Already, we're looking for new goals. You can't look back, only forward

James Lowes in the Don Valley dressing room

to the next challenge. Our burning desire is now to go through the league season undefeated. We've got three games to go, three hard games, but we'll have a go. Then there's the Premiership. We'll be having a shot at that. And surely a Bradford player must win the Man of Steel award.

"The overriding memory of that night in Sheffield, for me, will be my feelings as I looked around the stadium just before the game. To see so many Bradford people there with their flags and jerseys, willing the team to win, a great sense of anticipation in the air, was a humbling experience.

"It was real hard to contain my emotions. I realised, though I already knew it, that I was part of something special. And this is only the beginning."

Elliott managed to get the minds of his Bulls players back on playing when they reported back for training on Monday morning. The Super

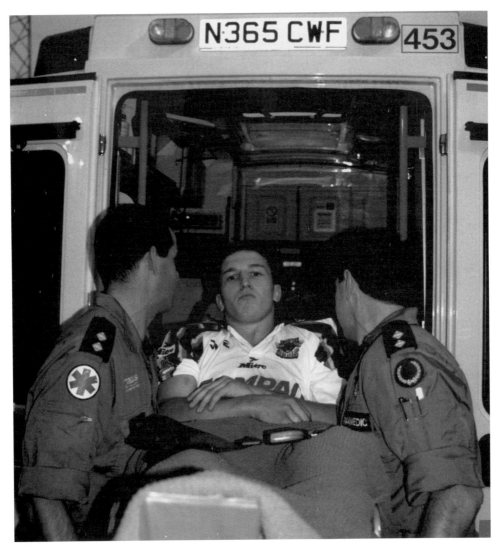

The celebrations against Paris were marred by a serious leg injury to winger Andy Hodgson, who left for hospital well before the end of the game.

League trophy hadn't been presented at Don Valley, the club and the RFL preferring to wait for the home game against Paris Saint-Germain.

The Bulls knew they had to serve up something special as a thank you to those fans who had roared them to the title-clinching win at Sheffield a week earlier, and they did not let them down. The Bulls rattled up a club record winning margin of 68-0.

Poor PSG played their part perfectly. They offered only token resistance and moved fastest when leaving Bradford to enjoy the post-match party while they hurried away from the ground even before the Champions were presented with the trophy.

For everyone else inside Odsal it was a marvellous night of celebration, with most of the 17,128 crowd still in the stadium almost an hour after the final whistle. They did not want it to end.

But amid all the jubilation Bradford loose forward Steve McNamara sounded a cautionary note about how St Helens had been enjoying the same acclaim a year earlier, and were now going through a rocky period.

"It's been a great night of celebrations, but we remember St Helens saying they were going to press on and be the force that Wigan had been," he recalled. "We are not going to make any rash statements, but if we keep the team together and build on what we've got I don't see why we can't have success for many years to come."

Danny Peacock had more reason than most to celebrate, charging in for his first hat-trick for the club. The Australian centre began the second half onslaught after Bradford had eased off in the first half to have only a modest 20-0 interval lead. He powered over from close range within two minutes of the restart, and added two more typical touchdowns as he hit the pass in full stride to blast through an unwilling defence.

Peacock also turned try creator when sending Gary Christie over, and there was no doubting his right to individual match honours. But James Lowes deserved some extra reward for another totally involved performance. The hooker is one of only four players to have appeared in every round since Super League was launched, and he showed no sign of easing up.

Apart from a brief spell to have stitches inserted into an eyebrow wound, there was no stopping Lowes as he slipped in for two tries and carved out another two - all from his play-the-ball lair. It's his natural habitat, as he burrows in and out, fetching and carrying to leave bewildered defences in total disarray. Short of smoking him out, it seems there is nothing they can do to control the pest.

Captain Robbie Paul was equally tantalising early on, as he dazzled the opposition in specially made £1,000 golden boots, and produced a superb pass to send Andy Hodgson sprinting 40 metres for a fourth minute touchdown. Starting at fullback for the first time in the senior side, Hodgson looked set for a big night, only for it all to cave in for him when he was stretchered off with a broken leg eleven minutes later.

The Champions' party did not take long to warm up, as Paul Loughlin scored the first try inside two minutes, and three more followed in the first quarter. Hodgson got his, Glen Tomlinson kicked through for another, and Jeff Wittenberg highlighted a tremendous first half performance with a 20th minute touchdown.

The Bulls then took a breather before really going to town in the second half with a ten-try romp that left Paris spinning. They were

virtually lining up to score, and none was more delighted when his turn came than former Dewsbury Rams winger Kevin Crouthers, when he was presented with a first try for the club.

Veteran substitute forward Paul Medley also looked pleased, as he helped himself to two, which tripled his total for the season but left him only three short of a career century for the club.

Have we forgotten anybody? Oh yes, Stuart Spruce also kept the party going with one. Had McNamara been in his usual kicking form Bradford would have soared past their record 76-0 victory over Leigh East amateurs in 1991, but this season's top goalscorer could manage only six.

It was, however, Bradford's widest winning margin against a senior club, and the victory equalled a club record of 21 successive league wins, having won their last Super League game of 1996.

Eventually it was time for the presentation. The Bulls left the field while technicians hurriedly assembled a stage in the centre of the field, and re-emerged wearing t-shirts emblazoned with the word 'champions' underneath the Bulls logo.

The Bullettes formed a guard of honour. A deafening noise, generated by the huge crowd, greeting the players back onto the field as they made their way towards the platform where the glittering trophy awaited. Robbie Paul hoisted Bradford's first major trophy in nearly two decades, and another party began to dwarf the one at Sheffield six days earlier.

Every player was cheered as the trophy was passed down the line, but the loudest cheer was reserved for Elliott. Joined on the pitch by his three daughters, he led the team on a slow lap of honour, soaking up the applause from the crowd.

He posed for pictures with everyone who wanted one, and after an hour managed to force his way though the crowds to the relative calm of the dressing room. Alone at last with his players and staff, he embraced assistants Brian Noble, Mick Potter and Carl Jennings, picked up a tin of beer and posed for even more photographs.

Noble was the only remaining connection to Bradford's last Championship-winning side. Later that night, at the official reception at nearby Cedar Court Hotel, he attempted to compare the two sides and highlighted the differences between then and now.

"The 1981 side was a physical, powerful one with forwards like Jimmy Thompson and Jeff Grayshon, who were colossal in the pack," he recalled.

"I was the youngster, and was dictated to by the older blokes. But the

All smiles for Sonny Nickle and Paul Loughlin

character of the side was the same as today's, and we all worked for each other. There were two subs, not four, and we had 17 or 18 players all capable of first team football, so our squad strength was important.

"We were all working, so we trained on Tuesday and Thursday nights and played at weekends. Weight programmes were non-existent, though I remember Jimmy Thompson worked out with weights, and I was doing them on my own. We played a lot of touch rugby in training, and had a good social side. I remember there was a great team spirit, and we all got on with each other. For big games we tried to get an afternoon off work and fit in an extra training session."

Noble paused, thought for a moment, and then weighed up the talents of the two eras.

"If those players had played in this era, and had the benefit of full-time training, they'd have been just as successful. The team was full of tough, hard, rugged guys who could stand up and be counted when it mattered.

"Odsal was a cold hole, and we played and trained in snow, hail and rain, and on a notoriously bad pitch. Northern were a physical side who bashed up the opposition. It was often cold and miserable, but we were suited to the ground. It was worth twelve points start to us.

"But Odsal Stadium in summer is a sensational place. Super League has had a dramatic effect on the stadium's life expectancy. Coming out of the tunnel at the start of a game now I get a tingle down the back of my neck with the atmosphere. Odsal is a real daunting place to play. I'd hate to be an opposition player."

13

WINNING DOESN'T LAST FOREVER

WITH the Super League title wrapped up, the Bulls set their sights on a new target. No team had ever gone a full season without losing, but with just two games remaining even the sternest critics were admitting the Bulls looked unbeatable.

Achieving that aim would be tough. Wigan at home and London away stood between the Bulls and an incredible record that surely would never be beaten.

Games against Wigan at Odsal invariably live long in the memory. Who will ever forget the 6-7 Challenge Cup defeat in March 1985 when Henderson Gill broke Bradford hearts with a controversial match-winning try. He was so far in touch on his way to the line that Bradford fans claimed that he almost ran around the back of the main stand!

And who will forget the thrilling 31-30 Bradford victory in September 1990 and the tremendous push-over try from a scrum as the big Bradford pack drove the famed Wigan six back fully 20 yards.

The thousands on the Odsal terraces on August Bank Holiday Monday were hoping for another memorable victory. How sweet it would be to create another new record against the side that had dominated the game for over a decade. Now it was the Bulls turn to be number one. They were the new team to be feared.

After blasting to an 18-0 lead in the early stages, it appeared those hopes were about to be realised. Unfortunately, Wigan hadn't read the script and refused to be just another statistic on the Bulls record-breaking run. What they wanted more than anything, in a largely disappointing

Wigan's Gary Connolly wraps up Stuart Spruce as the Bulls go down to their first defeat of the season.

season by their exacting standards, was to be the team who finally brought the Bulls run to an abrupt end.

Just before half-time, they began to claw their way back into the game. Forty minutes later, they had secured a convincing 33-18 win.

Matthew Elliott found it hard to contain his emotion after the game.

"There are a few things that contributed to it, and perhaps a few scrap-books were weighing people down," he said.

"Wigan's enthusiasm and hunger in the second stanza was inspiring, but the biggest contributor to the result was Bradford. There are some players who have got question marks over them about their position in the team."

Elliott would not say who those players were, but made it clear that there was nothing wrong with Robbie Paul's fitness when he recalled Bradford's captain to the bench in the closing stages.

Jason Robinson was the Bulls' chief tormentor. He sensed that it would take something special to get Wigan back into the game, and he was the man to produce it. He followed the ball across field before shooting onto Andrew Farrell's pass to leave the home defence in tatters on a swerving 50-metre dash to the posts. Farrell added the goal to make it 6-18 at half-time, and tagged on another when Henry Paul scrambled through for a 54th minute touchdown.

Three minutes later Wigan were level, thanks to another piece of brilliance by Robinson, who this time raced 60 metres on an in and out glorious run to the line.

Farrell also played a major role in Wigan's revival. In addition to getting Robinson away for his first half try, he broke through in great style before sending in Neil Cowie for the final touchdown. Add seven goals, including a field-goal, and Farrell's contribution was immense.

Yet Bradford had been in total command early on, with Jon Scales scoring inside a minute, followed by tries from James Lowes and Bernard Dwyer. Lowes also had another claim for a try rejected after squeezing over from acting halfback. In his last two matches the hooker had now scored or created five tries, and had two more disallowed.

But whatever the reason, the long winning run had come to an end.

It was always going to happen eventually, but when it did it hurt players and supporters alike. There was still a record up for grabs though, and victory at London on the Sunday would mean just one defeat from the whole campaign.

Elliott decided to take his entire squad south, travelling down Friday and staying in the capital for three nights, such was his determination to end the season on a high. The vast army of Bulls supporters wanted to be there too, and thousands made the long haul down the M1 as though the game was a cup final, not merely the final hurdle in a long season whose result mattered not to the final placings.

But the immaculate preparation couldn't prevent another defeat, and the Bulls went down 28-24 in a thrilling finale to the Super League season played out before a live television audience. The Broncos had finished the season as the form side and their emergence as a major force was confirmed with the win.

The game was played amid the gloom hanging over the nation following the sad death of Diana, Princess of Wales, in the early hours of the day. Chris Caisley joined Broncos chairman Barry Maranta and director Richard Branson on the field before the start of the game for two minutes' silence in memory of the Princess.

Despite the defeat and the sombre mood, it was a day of celebration for the thousands of Bulls' fans who invaded the capital and chanted "Bring on the Champions" after the game.

They shook the Stoop with their cheers when the Bulls got off to a great start, Mike Forshaw's pass setting Graeme Bradley off on a 50-metre run for the opening try.

Bradley then turned from hero to villain when a misplaced pass was picked up by Terry Matterson who sent Shaun Edwards running clear ito the corner, just evading Stuart Spruce's despairing tackle. Edwards played a major part in London's second try four minutes later when Martin Offiah announced his return after a six game absence by following his former Wigan teammate's kick through to touch down, just managing to avoid going into touch.

The Bulls were stung into action and hit back when Glen Tomlinson surged downfield. He offloaded to Spruce, Robbie Beazley went too high, and the Great Britain full-back shrugged him away for an impressive score. Robbie Paul set up Bernard Dwyer beautifully for another try, but Bawden and Beazley put the Broncos back in front.

Then the video referee controversially came to the Broncos aid to disallow a Tomlinson effort when James Lowes was adjudged to have knocked on while kicking through. It brought howls of protests from the terracing, but the players simply got on with the job and 90 seconds later found the line again, when a sweeping move ended with Danny Peacock sending in Paul Loughlin.

The pulsating game was levelled again by a Steve McNamara penalty to lock the score at 24-24, but McNamara's boot let him down when he tried a 30 metre field-goal just before the end.

A piece of brilliance from Edwards four minutes from time finally settled the game, sending a pass out wide with the Bulls at full stretch for Mardon to provide the final link to Offiah, who cut inside Spruce.

Steve McNamara looks to offload against Wigan

The Bulls staged one last ditch effort, but when referee Connolly pulled them back for a forward pass it all got too much for James Lowes who was sin binned for arguing.

All the talk in the bar after the game centred around the controversial decision to disallow Tomlinson's try. RFL Referees' Controller Geoff Berry later confirmed that the decision was in accordance with the rules of the game in relation to knock-ons and drop-kicks. The 'try' had been scored when Lowes received a pass, dropped the ball in front of his foot, kicked the ball forward immediately after it bounced, picked up and fed Tomlinson, who went over for what he thought was four points.

"A drop kick occurs when a ball is dropped for the purpose of being kicked," said Berry. "In this case, the way I saw it, the player in possession lost control of the ball, and then he kicked the ball as a response to losing it. Clearly that was a knock-on. I should point out that the match referee, John Connolly, said that he would have blown for a knock-on if he hadn't had the benefit of the video referee."

With the Super League campaign wrapped up, the end-of-season Premiership offered a new opportunity to win more silverware. The play-offs had suddenly become more important, following the two defeats to Wigan and London. The Bulls' critics were having a field day, and success at Old Trafford would re-affirm the Bulls' status.

Much of Matthew Elliott's time in the lead up to the first play-off against Castleford was taken by another simmering row between club and country for Robbie Paul. The Bulls skipper had been called up to play for New Zealand against Australia in Auckland, just two days before the Premiership Final. The Bulls were reluctant to lose their star man for such a big game should they qualify.

They called upon RFL chief executive Maurice Lindsay to exert his influence.

"As Chairman of the International Board I have to support the principle of international rugby," explained Lindsay. "This I do, but I have asked the New Zealand authorities to consider a proposition which may provide a route out of the problem. We have said that we are prepared to release Robbie's elder brother Henry for Test duty. If Bradford and Wigan win their respective rounds this weekend, they will face each other in the Premiership semi-finals. Whichever brother lost out on a Premiership final placing would be released to play for his country."

Lindsay made the point to New Zealand that Robbie Paul was released to play in the World Nines, and then in the ANZAC Day Test a week before the Silk Cut Challenge Cup Final.

"We don't think it is fair that Robbie should be denied the chance to play for his club in a major final. I have pointed out that this Test was not on the calendar when our big match fixtures were planned. It was not until two months ago that this fixture was first put in place.

"I've no doubt that Robbie will be disappointed because he would like to take part in both events, but having played all season for his club, it would seem against the spirit of what has happened."

The Bulls were also angry at being told their World Club Championship quarter-final in Auckland had been brought forward 48 hours to the Friday night after Old Trafford. Should the Bulls win through to the final it would mean they would arrive in Auckland just two days before the game.

"We might as well forfeit the game," fumed Elliott. "It's a ludicrous situation and shows just how seriously the British clubs are bring taken in this competition. Travelling all that way takes its toll on players, and this decision does little for the status of the competition."

And to complete a trio of problems for the club, newspaper reports suggested there was unrest in the Bulls camp. It was too much for Chris Caisley, who reacted angrily

"There are a lot of jealous people who would love to see us fall from grace, but I can assure our supporters that it won't happen," he blasted. "I wondered how long it would take for someone to have a go at upsetting the applecart."

The reports suggested senior players, including club captain Graeme Bradley, were unhappy with negotiations for new contracts.

"Graeme Bradley signed a new deal earlier this year that takes him through to the end of 1998, so I just cannot understand why anyone would report differently. We have one or two players whose contracts are up this year, but they don't expire till December. Before then we have the Premiership and World Club Championship to play for, and that is what everyone at the club is focussed on."

Caisley also denied that players were unhappy with their pay and bonuses.

"We have paid out in excess of £180,000 in bonus payments this year, and as for saying our players earn modest salaries, if I revealed our salary structure to the outside world no-one would regard it as modest. We want to be the best club in the world. But we won't fall into the same trap as other clubs who have won a competition and then spent all their money without reinvesting for the future.

"We are continuing to grow our business, and are currently looking at several exciting off-field projects that will be sensational. We will substantially increase our turnover to protect us from market forces. An increased turnover means a bigger salary cap."

Back on the field, the Bulls were preparing for the visit of the Tigers. Threatened with relegation all year, the Tigers had finally come good to avoid the drop and pick up some useful wins. They were quietly cocky of causing an upset.

"They are playing well at the moment and are much improved from earlier in the season," agreed Steve McNamara.

"Stuart Raper (Castleford coach) has done a great job without changing many of the players. He's got them playing mistake-free football and, now the worry of relegation has gone, they are playing with a lot more confidence. The win at Halifax last week will have been a big boost for them."

McNamara had an explanation for the Bulls' poor finale to the league campaign.

"The ruthless streak that we've had all season is missing. We were 18-0 up against Wigan and 18-6 up against London. From that situation we should have gone on to win both games. We played well in parts but took our foot off the gas too soon. The unbeaten tag meant a lot to us and we were all very disappointed to lose it.

"The London game was difficult because of the tragic events that morning. We didn't know whether the game would be on or off, but that's not an excuse because the circumstances were exactly the same for the Broncos.

Brian McDermott is well contained by a trio of Castleford Tigers.

"Now the Premiership is a different competition and everyone starts again. We want to win it more now than ever. Other sides have seen that we can be beaten and they will feel we are going through a sticky patch. I'm sure Castleford will fancy their chances, but we all had last week off for a complete rest and came back on Monday with our batteries recharged. It's been a long season and there's hopefully still a few weeks left for us yet."

Robbie Paul echoed McNamara's comments, and attempted to turn the two defeats into positives.

"It's important to have losses," he reflected. "Then you know how important wins are. If you won all the time you wouldn't know any different. I think that the defeats we had at Wembley and in the World Club Challenge stood us in good stead.

"We bounced back from those and really charged into the league competition. And these last two losses we have had against London and Wigan will put us in good stead for the play-offs. We are very hungry and we have had the play-offs in mind since we lifted the Super League trophy, because that is the next best thing.

"I think we got to a stage where everyone expected us to have big wins, but there is nothing better than beating a top side and knocking them off their pedestal. Every team picks itself up for those games. It is plain and simple. We lost and were out-played. Who is to say we even thought about going through unbeaten anyway?"

Those two defeats became three as Castleford produced a solid all-round team effort to dump the Bulls out of the Premiership. Suddenly, the worries about Paul playing for New Zealand and the Bulls not arriving in Auckland until just before the World Club Championship quarter-final with the Warriors, were insignificant.

It just wasn't the Bulls day. They suffered a pre-match blow when Graeme Bradley withdrew through injury and Matt Calland was sent off in the twelfth minute following a clash with Castleford's Chris Smith. The Tigers winger objected to Calland's tackle after he fielded a high kick and Calland responded with a straight punch. Down went Smith and off went Calland.

Hampered by this double blow, the Bulls fell well below their Championship form, apart from the occasional flashing run from Robbie Paul and Mike Forshaw, who highlighted a powerful second row display with a try and was unlucky to be disallowed another.

They struggled to get their attack going until just before half-time, when James Lowes slipped in for a trademark try from a play the ball, and Paul Loughlin's goal made it 8-11 at the interval. Within two minutes of the restart two more players were on the way to the sin bin following a brief flare-up - Bradford's Danny Peacock and Castleford's Adrian Vowles. Castleford got the penalty and another for a play the ball offence a few minutes later, and when Smith added a try the Bulls found themselves 8-19 down and in serious trouble.

For a while they started to hit something like their championship form. Peacock was prominent with a rousing mid-field run and they maintained the pressure for Forshaw to go charging over for a try on the hour, but it wasn't enough to get past the resurgent Tigers.

The defeat left the Bulls with one final chance of adding to the Super League title, and they headed to Auckland on what appeared to be mission impossible.

The night before jetting off on yet another long distance trip, the Bulls had been at the Holiday Inn Crowne Plaze in Manchester for the annual

Stones Man of Steel Dinner. It is the social highlight of the Rugby League year, a glittering ceremony where the top accolades in the game are handed out. The Bulls were favourites to land at least two of the prizes and had reserved a couple of tables to accommodate their large and expectant party.

They weren't disappointed. The whole evening seemed to have a Bulls theme running through it, from the opening scenes on the huge video wall, through a special tribute to the Champions, and the eventual announcement of the winners.

Matthew Elliott scooped the Coach of the Year ahead of Salford's Andy Gregory and London's Tony Currie, and James Lowes collected the double. First, he was voted the Super League Player of the Year by his fellow professionals and then he picked up the ultimate individual award, the prestigious Stones Man of Steel.

"I had no idea I was going to win, and I'm very surprised," Lowes told the audience.

"It's one of the highlights of my career. It's a reflection of what the team has achieved, and I have to give credit to Matthew and the coaching staff. I wish I could have dozens of these trophies to give to each individual at the club, because everyone has worked so hard.

"The highlight was picking up the trophy against Paris, but the game that I'll always remember was at Halifax away. We were well down at half-time, but came out to show what real character and determination we have. I never thought about winning the title or individual awards like this. I literally took each game as it came, and tried to keep on track week by week.

"I'm enjoying my game now better than ever. When I was at Leeds the Bradford fans hated me, but now it's the other way round! The fans have been great, and there is a special feeling at Odsal.

Elliott also dedicated his award to the whole club.

"I see this as recognition of what the club has achieved, more than what I have done at a personal level. I'm proud to be recognised in this way, but it's down to the organisation's efforts as a whole, the confidence the board showed in me, and the support and vision they have shown since.

"Brian Smith has had a big contribution in me reaching this level, and I've had the skill and expertise of my staff Michael Potter, Brian Noble and Carl Jennings.

"But the people I want to acknowledge most of all are my players. They are an outstanding group of people who were prepared to work hard. They might not have liked everything that was asked of them, but they did it.

James Lowes and Matthew Elliott celebrate with their
awards at the Stones Man of Steel dinner.

"You don't think about winning things like this. It's good to win and I feel warm and fuzzy about it, but if it was a choice between getting the coach of the year or winning things as a team, there's no choice.

"I believe we are the team to beat, and in most areas we have proved that, but there are still a lot of things we need to prove. The big thing for us now is dealing with success. We haven't coped with it particularly well this time, and when we crossed the finishing line our lap of honour was a poor one.

"It's been invaluable for me to look back on those defeats at the end of the season. It hurt like hell at the time, and I was very unhappy, but I've learnt from it, and next time we encounter it we will all be better prepared. Not many of us have experienced the kind of success we've had, and the euphoria that surrounded it all was emotionally draining.

"We're well and truly over it now, and we are going to Auckland with

Robbie Paul hauled down at Auckland.

a purpose. Tonight has put a bit of energy in me, and there are a few more beans in the can. I believe the coach sets the standard for the rest of the team, so hopefully my renewed energy will rub off on them during the next few days."

The celebratory champagne flowed until the early hours, but at seven o'clock Elliott, Lowes and the rest of the Bulls were on their way to Manchester Airport.

Nobody needed reminding of the last time the Bulls set foot on New Zealand soil. Auckland 64 Bradford 14, the scoreline spoke for itself, but Robbie Paul was more eager than most to prove that defeat was a one-off. He linked up with the squad again Down Under after playing for New Zealand in their superb Test win against Australia, a win that had the Kiwi buzzing.

"I enjoyed the Test Match enormously. It was one of the best moments of my Rugby League career. I was only on for fifteen minutes, but they were the best fifteen minutes of my life."

There was a theory that the Auckland players, coming back into the World Club Championship after an eight week lay-off, would be ring rusty and that match-fit Bradford would be in prime position to take advantage.

"The Test was an awesome experience. I know I had a try disallowed, but I can't think of the match in individual terms at all. It was a great team effort, and most of those guys will be facing us on Friday. I'm sure I can give Matthew and the boys a few insights into the blokes I was playing with, but you can't really teach people about other players until they experience coming up against their talents for themselves."

Paul knew he would have his hands full opposing his Kiwi team-mate Stacey Jones.

"Stacey is going to be a freak, if he isn't one already. He's got great skills, he's lightning off the mark, and can beat anybody in a short sprint. Stacey is a sensational player.

"It's not just at scrum-half, though, the Warriors have talent coming at you from all sides. But we haven't come out here looking for more of the

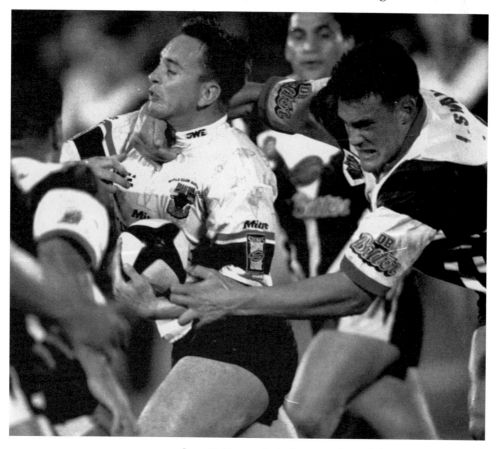

Steve McNamara looks for a way through the Auckland Warriors.

Kevin Crouthers holds his head in despair as Auckland rattle up another huge score

same, we're going to compete this time. The finish to our season was a bit of a damp squib, and we're looking to put that right. I feel good, the lads feel good. We know we've got a tough job to do, but we're up for it.

"We are European Super League champions after all, and nobody can ever take that away from us."

Despite all their predictions, the Bulls went down by another similarly huge score. By the end of a game which had been littered with errors from both sides, the Aucklanders were ridiculing the European Champions.

They gave up territory with a series of short, rugby union-style kick-offs; Matthew Ridge tried a sideline conversion with his left foot, and then allowed non-kicking winger Sean Hoppe to toe-hack the final attempt below the crossbar.

Matthew Elliott found himself in no position to complain about the blatant disrespect.

"That was nobody's fault but our own," Elliott admitted. "They wouldn't have treated us with a lack of respect if we had only been six or twelve points behind.

"We lacked the discipline to our game. It's a disappointing way to finish the season, but it was our 39th game. There were a lot of tired and busted players out there."

There were, however, at least two outstanding competitors in the visiting line-up who didn't deserve to be made into laughing stocks.

Second-rower Mike Forshaw and forward replacement Paul Medley ripped into the Aucklanders, and almost embarrassed the home pack with their first half work rate and commitment.

Forshaw in particular stood out, as he had done for most of the season. His reward was a first call-up to the Great Britain squad, a remarkable turnaround for a player who six months' earlier was out of Rugby League.

"It has been a wonderful way to get back into the game, and it has gone better than I could have imagined," said Forshaw.

"Regardless of what happened in the final weeks, it has been a great year. When you keep winning it becomes harder to imagine losing. Our confidence was high, everyone thought we could do something special, and we achieved it.

"We never gave in, even when we were down, as at Halifax, when we kept our unbeaten record after we'd been well down.

"I've always been confident in my ability, and here it brings the best out of you, with the crowd and the atmosphere it generates."

14
INTO THE FUTURE

TOWARDS the end of the season, with the title firmly secured, the Bulls began to look to the future. Rugby League had changed so much since the inception of Super League, and there will be many more changes to come.

In anticipation of further re-structuring within the game, and always keen to lead the way, Chris Caisley and his Bulls launched an innovative link-up with neighbours Dewsbury Rams in a unique partnership to develop amateur players and coaches.

Titled the 'Bulls-Rams Association', the two clubs will pool resources and manpower in creating a pyramid structure that has been hailed as the blueprint for the future of Rugby League.

RFL Technical Director Joe Lydon welcomed the initiative.

"When we began to look at ways of raising standards, we realised very early on that unless you encourage youth development there is no future for the game," he said.

"Some tough decisions have to be made, and it's encouraging that two organisations have shown the vision and foresight to ignore the insular thinking that has prevented the game from fulfiling its massive potential."

Amateur clubs throughout the Bradford and Dewsbury catchment area are now being invited to join the association.

"Our aim is to enhance the development of the game, with specific benefits being passed on to junior clubs within the association," explained Bulls' spokesman Steve Fairhurst.

"Member clubs will be assisted with all aspects of grass roots development and the attainment of excellence."

The scheme creates a structured career path for young players and coaches, from under 8's level right through to eventual Bulls first grade and beyond for the most successful.

Specialised coaching will be on offer to member clubs, along with assistance off the field for projects involving grant applications.

All players under 16 will be offered free season tickets, and greater levels of compensation will be paid to clubs whose players are signed on professional terms by the Bull or the Rams.

There will be an immediate £250 signing on fee, another £250 if he joins the Rams, a further £250 if he joins the Bulls and another £500 when he has made ten appearances for the Bulls.

In the shorter term, the link-up also offers Bulls' current reserve-grade players and those returning from injury a better level of competition.

"I have a squad of 25 players, which means there are seven disappointed guys every week," said Bulls' coach Matthew Elliott.

"At the moment they go into the Alliance team, where the benefit is minimal. I would much prefer to see them playing for Dewsbury in the First Division.

"Recently I had Jeremy Donougher and Robbie Paul coming back from injury. Jeremy played in the Alliance side, and I risked Robbie in the first team, which was a little premature.

"Just think of the benefit to the Dewsbury club if Robbie Paul turned out in a Dewsbury shirt!"

Rams coach Neil Kelly is also excited by the partnership.

"I was very sceptical at first, but there are so many positives," he said.

"I'm excited by the prospect. As we progress ideas will develop because we are all working together and want to get as high up as we can."

Over 50,000 youngsters will have been coached by the Bulls by the end of this year, and much of the Association's aims are aimed at youth development.

"We recently studied the Australian method of developing young players," explained one of the Bulls' development officers, Darrall Shelford.

"We were impressed by how closely the professional clubs work with the amateurs and that is obviously an area we need to work on.

"We shouldn't just rely on a child's natural ability. We should develop that ability from an early age.

"Every amateur coach gives up a lot in terms of time, energy and commitment and we want to give them the back-up they need. We don't want to dictate, but it's important that we put more emphasis on teaching skills.

"I'm often amazed at how many 16 year-olds can't pass a ball or tackle properly. Through the Association we can ensure that when a youngster

Shaun Edwards eyes the Super League trophy as Chris Caisley
announces his signing at a packed press conference

gets to Academy level we don't have to re-educate him."

As well as ensuring the grassroots of the game in the Bulls catchment area were well catered for, the Bulls moved to strengthen their top squad with the arrival of Shaun Edwards on a two year contract from London Broncos.

The former Wigan great, now 30, had been one of the key players in London's best ever season that saw them finish runners-up to the Bulls in Super League.

"Shaun's signing will lead us forward into the next stage of our development," said a delighted Chris Caisley at the packed press conference to announce his signing.

"Our ambitions are without limits, but one is to become the number one club in the world. This is another massive step towards achieving that ambition. Shaun is the best halfback in the British game, bar none. His record speaks for itself. He's a winner, an inspirational player, and we're absolutely delighted to welcome him on board."

Edwards himself was at pains to stress that he had left the Broncos on amicable terms, but was looking forward to his latest challenge.

"I've had a good season with London, but when a champion club like Bradford Bulls is interested in you, you have to sit up and take notice," he said.

"I take it as a great compliment. I've always fancied playing at Odsal. The atmosphere has whetted my appetite when I have been in opposition here, and I'm just glad I'm playing for the Bulls now instead of against them."

"I've looked at the squad, and I haven't seen one player who has come to Bradford and got worse. Hopefully I'm not going to be the first. I want to improve. Previously unknown players have come here and become internationals. There must be something in the coaching set-up responsible for that, and it was another big factor behind my decision.

"The secret of that Wigan side was that they were never happy with what they'd got. They always wanted to be better. From what I've seen so far, the Bulls have that same attitude."

But Edwards arrival didn't go down well with everybody. Glen Tomlinson was so dismayed at the signing that he refused to travel to Auckland for the final game of the season, immediately casting a huge cloud over his future at Odsal. The dispute was not resolved as this book went to print.

Further signings and departures were planned, and Paul Loughlin was transfer-listed along with Gary Christie.

"You have to weigh up what is best for the future of the club," said Elliott. "It's like allowing Paul Cook to leave earlier in the season. That was a tough decision but I don't regret it. I will be sad to see Paul Loughlin leave, too. His contribution to this club has been far more than what you see on gameday. He's irreplaceable as far as building team spirit is concerned but, in the end, I believe we have made the right decision. I can't always be fair but I always try to be honest. There is no easy way of telling a player he doesn't have a future at the club, and you can understand it when they feel bitter.

"I've been there myself. Rejection is hard to take. Paul hasn't missed a training session since he's been here and he has further to travel than most. He's a special individual.

"But we have a squad of 26 and we need to bring in new, younger blood. The squad can't keep growing, there has to be a turnover of players. There will be others leaving, too. We need to look at our three-quarters and bring in a bit of pace. Matt Calland has had a quiet season by his standards, Locker's is leaving and I see Graeme Bradley moving into the pack next season.

"In bringing in new players we can't compromise the qualities that we have such as size and power. We haven't had to rely on running 70 metres for our tries this year. We have managed to build our technique well and get close in because of the way we play. But without doubt pace is a quality we need to add.

"I have two recruitment conditions that I stand by. One is character, the other is quality. Our forward strength is good, but it would be nice to add more quality to our backline. That is not to say we don't already have quality in those positions, but we need to make subtle adjustments.

"Whether the players are out there or not is another question, and that is why we are starting to build our younger home-grown players up. We have some good sixteen and seventeen year-olds, and some good twenty-somethings. We need to build on the eighteen and nineteen year-olds.

Caisley, too, refused to allow emotion get in the way of his determination to move on to bigger and better things in years to come.

"What we would like to do is add a couple of quality players, and we have already been looking at that very hard," he said.

"We are in the process of improving our training facilities and junior development will certainly be improving with the formation of the Bulls/Rams Association.

"In terms of marketing we also have a lot of things up our sleeves, and sponsorship and merchandising are running at record levels. Our merchandising operation has grossed in excess of £750,000 this year. That's gone from £100,000 two years ago, and is a reflection of the brand loyalty we now have. All the signs are that the great season we have had is producing the sort of knock-on effects we hoped for."

"You always have to set yourself goals. Since 1995 our motto has been to reach for the skies and see how far we can go. We were told we would never make summer rugby work or attract youngsters to our ground, but we have been single-minded and just got on and achieved it.

"Now I certainly think average crowds of 17,000 are highly achievable. I also think 20,000 on a regular basis is not beyond the bounds of possibility. Certainly the message going out for people wanting to sit in the stands next season is to buy a season ticket or they won't get in.

"For the bigger games too, I think there is a possibility of the 'sell-out' signs being put up. It's a far cry from the days when the club was attracting 4-5,000 fans. Looking back they were pretty dark days but I always knew where I wanted us to be and, despite a lot of frustrations, we never lost sight of that. That in many ways is the most satisfying part of this season's success.

"It is not often in life you sit down and set out a strategy, set about implementing it and see it produce results more quickly than you planned for. This was no fluke. From the man who opens the turnstiles on gameday right through to the Board, everyone has played their part."

The one black spot is the continued doubts over the future of the stadium and the proposed Superdome development.

"It is the one thing we have no control over. It is a millstone round our necks and is causing us to lose £500,000 a year. When you consider that, 1997 really has been a fabulous achievement by all concerned at the club."

As the Bulls squad began to break up for a few weeks' well deserved rest, Elliott was in an upbeat mood as he reflected on the long but rewarding season of nearly 40 punishing games since February.

"We have had a big season, which retrospectively was a really a huge success, and it is now important that everybody recharges their batteries ready for an even tougher campaign next season. The players will not be called back to training until early November, and by then I hope they will all have fully recovered form the knocks, bruises and bangs that they have picked up, and that they will be ready and raring to go again.

"The defeats after we won the title did take the shine off things a little, but it has been a hard season, we had achieved our objective, and perhaps the euphoria of it all just got to us too much. The schedule of fixtures did take its toll, and although I would have expected us to come out of the trip to Auckland with more credit, I have to be realistic and say that it was a big ask for us to get anything from that game after the effort that had been put into our season.

"We had played ten more games than our Australasian counterparts,

Chris Caisley at a Bulls planning meeting with (FROM LEFT)
Stephen Coulby, Gary Tasker, Colin Tordoff and Jack Bates.

and over the length of a season that takes its toll.

The Australasian sides are that much stronger than us. But in the early rounds of the World Championship that was not particularly an issue for us. We competed well, and were unlucky not to win at least two of our home games.

"But by the time of the second round we were cramming games in, and the sheer volume of what we had to play was bound to take its toll. There are three main cycles necessary for a player to give an optimum performance. They are recovery, preparation and then playing. But the only one you cannot cut down on is the recovery cycle.

"Players need a set amount of time to get over the rigours of their last match. Because that factor is pretty constant, you then cut down on preparation to get other games in, and gradually it wears the players down. I had hoped that we would have gone better in the World Club Championship play-off, but we were very tired by then, and the loss of recovery over the preceding weeks meant that our reserves were not great enough to contain Auckland. We were in the game for the first half, but fell away badly.

"That is an area that we shall be trying to address for next season, and I am going to Philadelphia Eagles in November to study their preparation techniques.

"Next season, it will be harder than ever, because the Bulls will be the side that everyone will want to beat. We will have to work harder than ever to make sure we stay at the top."

Caisley agreed with Elliott, and refused to shy away from the task ahead.

"We know next season is going to be even tougher so we have to get better. It is up to the coach and the Board to procure the players we need to do that.

"We will certainly be giving it our best shot."

APPENDIX 1
THE CAST

THE MANAGEMENT

PRESIDENT
COLIN TORDOFF
Recently sold his Bradford-based textile company, Cowper & Tordoff, to a major international organisation. Now Managing Director of the Bulls, he is responsible for ensuring board policy is implemented.

CHAIRMAN
CHRIS CAISLEY
Chairman since 1989, Caisley is a senior partner for Leeds law firm Walker Morris. He is vice consul to the Netherlands and a former director of the Rugby Football League. He is currently chairman of Rugby League (Europe) Ltd.

DIRECTORS;
JACK BATES
Chairman of Bradford prior to Caisley. Retired from the family building and plumbing company in Bradford, he is responsible for stadium and ground issues.

ROLAND AGAR
Ilkley butcher who first got involved with Bradford when he helped fund the Deryck Fox transfer, then a record fee. His board duties include looking after youth development for the club.

STEPHEN COULBY
Harrogate-based, works in the corporate hospitality business. Has been on the board for two years and is in charge of marketing.

THE COACHING STAFF

HEAD COACH: MATTHEW ELLIOTT

Born:	8th December 1964 at Thursday Island, Queensland
Height:	183cm
Weight:	95kg
Nickname:	Mattie
Marital Status:	To Karen. Three Children. Mia 7, Lucy-Anne 5, Claire 2.
Contracted:	1995 as Assistant Coach to Brian Smith; 1996 as Head Coach
Previous Clubs:	St George
Rep. Honours:	Playing in Winfield Cup Grand Final 1992, won the French Cup & Championship in 1988. Also played cricket for Australian Schoolboys Honorary Team
Career Highlight:	Being a part of Wembley in 1996 and 1997
Career Ambition:	As a child I always wanted to play Rugby League and Cricket for Australia. Now I want to see the Bulls realise their true potential
Hobbies:	Golf and my family

ASSISTANT COACH: BRIAN DAVID NOBLE

Born:	14th February 1961 in Bradford
Height:	170cm
Weight:	86kg
Nickname:	Nobby
Marital Status:	Married to Barbara, with 2 children
Previous Clubs:	Cronulla, Wakefield Trinity
Rep. Honours:	Great Britain, Yorkshire
Career Highlight:	Great Britain captain on 1984 Australian Tour
Career Ambition:	To coach Great Britain against Australia and win
Hobbies:	Motorbikes, trying to keep fit

ASSISTANT COACH: MICHAEL POTTER

Born:	24th September, 1963 at Parramatta, NSW
Height:	176cm
Weight:	80kg
Nickname:	Potts

Marital Status:	Married to Megan
Previous Clubs:	St George (1988-93), Canterbury (1983-88), Perth (1995-96)
Rep. Honours:	NSW (1984), City (1986), Country (1990, 1991, 1992)
Career Highlight:	Four Grand Finals, twice a winner of the Dally M Medal.
Hobbies:	Golf and Tennis

HEAD CONDITIONER: CARL JENNINGS

Born:	4th May 1965 at Hull
Height:	183cm
Weight:	108kg
Nickname:	Jeno
Marital Status:	Married
Rep. Honours:	GB International Athlete
Career Highlight:	British Champion Shot Putt
Career Ambition:	Help the Bulls to become world number one
Hobbies:	Keep fit, power development, DIY

THE PLAYERS

JOHN PAUL ANDERSON

Born:	25th October 1971 at Castleford
Height:	185cm
Weight:	121kg
Marital Status:	Married to Lisa
Position:	Prop
Contracted:	March 1997
Previous Clubs:	Halifax (1993-97), Leeds (1989-93)
Rep. Honours:	BARLA under-19, Great Britain under-21
Career Highlight:	Signing for the Bradford Bulls
Career Ambition:	To win every major trophy with the Bulls
Hobbies:	Golf, squash, and badminton

GRAEME JOHN BRADLEY

Born:	20th March 1964 at Sydney, NSW, Australia
Height:	187cm
Weight:	99kg
Nickname:	Penguin

Marital Status:	Single
Position:	Centre or stand-off
Contracted:	August, 1995
Previous Clubs:	St George (1993-95), Penrith (1988-1991), Castleford (1991-92), Illawarra (1985-87)
Rep. Honours:	City Firsts (1989), Australian XIII v Great Britain (1988)
Career Highlight:	Playing in the 1993 Winfield Cup Grand Final with St George
Career Ambition:	To win the Challenge Cup
Hobbies:	Reading, going to the races

MATTHEW HUGH CALLAND

Born:	20 August 1971 at Widnes
Height:	183 cm
Weight:	100 kg
Marital Status:	Single
Position:	Centre
Contracted:	November, 1995
Previous Clubs:	Featherstone Rovers (1993-95), Rochdale (1990-93)
Rep. Honours:	Lancashire under-19, Great Britain under-19
Career Highlight:	Winning last year's Challenge Cup semi-final
Career Ambition:	To win the Challenge Cup
Hobbies:	Computer games, football, overseas travel

GARY CHRISTIE

Born:	23rd January 1972 at Birkenhead
Height:	177cm
Weight:	86kg
Nickname:	Christmas, Back Flip
Marital Status:	Single
Contracted:	November, 1994
Position:	Fullback, centre or wing
Previous Clubs:	Wakefield Trinity (1993-94), Oldham (1991-93)
Rep. Honours:	BARLA under-19, Lancashire under-19, Great Britain under-21
Career Highlight:	Winning last year's Challenge Cup semi-final
Hobbies:	Sailing, fishing, and playing video games

PAUL IAN COOK

Born:	23rd July 1976 at Hull
Height:	177cm

Weight:	89kg
Nickname:	Cookie
Marital Status:	Single
Position:	Wing or fullback
Contracted:	December, 1995 (left May 1996)
Previous Clubs:	Leeds (1992-95)
Rep. Honours:	Yorkshire under-19, Great Britain under-19, Great Britain under-21, England (2 caps in 1995 World Cup)
Career Highlight:	Playing for England in the World Cup

KEVIN PAUL CROUTHERS

Born:	3rd January 1976 at Wakefield
Height:	185cm
Weight:	94kg
Nickname:	Kenny
Marital Status:	Single
Position:	Centre or wing
Contracted:	May 1997
Previous Clubs:	Dewsbury
Career Highlight:	Last minute field-goal to beat Featherstone 17-16
Career Ambition:	To play for Great Britain
Hobbies:	Weight training, Pool, Motorcross Racing

JEREMY ALAN DONOUGHER

Born:	28th November 1969 at Pambula, NSW, Australia
Height:	191 cm
Weight:	110 kg
Nickname:	Jed
Marital Status:	Married to Eileen
Position:	Second row
Contracted:	August, 1995
Previous Clubs:	South Sydney (1993-95), St George (1989-92)
Rep. Honours:	NSW Open Schoolboys, Australian Open Schoolboys
Career Highlight:	Winning the ARL under-21 Grand Final and the 1994 Tooheys Challenge
Career Ambition:	To win the Challenge Cup with the Bulls
Hobbies:	Golf, horse racing and tennis

BERNARD JOHN DWYER

Born:	20th April 1969 at St Helens

Height:	175cm
Weight:	98kg
Nickname:	Barney
Marital Status:	Married to Jackie
Position:	Second row
Contracted:	November, 1995
Previous Clubs:	St Helens (1984-95)
Rep. Honours:	Great Britain Colts, Ireland, Great Britain (including the 1996 tour to Papua New Guinea, Fiji, and New Zealand)
Career Highlight:	Winning the 1993 Premiership Final with St Helens and the 1997 Super League with Bradford
Career Ambition:	To win the Silk Cut Challenge Cup
Hobbies:	Golf, and spending time with my wife and three children

ABI CHIEDU EKOKU

Born:	13th April 1966 in London
Height:	187cm
Weight:	100kg
Marital Status:	Single
Position:	Wing
Contracted:	January, 1997
Previous Clubs:	Halifax (1995-96), London Broncos (1993-95)
Rep. Honours:	England (athletics, including selection for the1990 Commonwealth Games in Auckland, New Zealand) and Great Britain (athletics again, including selection for the 1990 European Championships in Split, Croatia)
Career Highlight:	Signing for Bradford Bulls and winning the Super League
Career Ambition:	To win the Challenge Cup
Hobbies:	Football, athletics, literature, and music

MICHAEL FORSHAW

Born:	5th January 1970 at Wigan
Height:	180cm
Weight:	95kg
Nickname:	Forsh
Marital Status:	Married to Vicky with baby Rory
Position:	Back row
Contracted:	April, 1997

Previous Clubs:	Wigan, Leeds, Saracens RU
Rep. Honours:	Great Britain under-21, Great Britain
Career Highlight:	Beating Penrith with Wigan in the 1991 World Club Challenge
Hobbies:	Spending time with my baby, reading

NATHAN JAMES GRAHAM

Born:	23rd November 1971 at Bristol
Height:	175cm
Weight:	84kg
Nickname:	Grash
Marital Status:	Engaged to Jane
Position:	Stand-off or fullback
Contracted:	June, 1995
Previous Clubs:	Dewsbury (1988-95)
Career Highlight:	Beating Leeds in the 1996 Challenge Cup semi-final, winning the 1997 Super League
Career Ambition:	To cement a regular place in the Bulls team
Hobbies:	Golf, cricket, and looking after Joshua, my 18-month-old son

ANDY HODGSON

Born:	9th February 1976 at Keighley
Height:	177cm
Weight:	83kg
Marital Status:	Single
Position:	Fullback
Contracted:	May, 1997
Previous Clubs:	Wharfedale RUFC.
Rep. Honours:	Yorkshire under-19, 21. North England under-21
Career Highlight:	Playing at Twickenham for Yorkshire under-21

WARREN SCOTT JOWITT

Born:	9th September 1974 at Crofton, Wakefield
Height:	185cm
Weight:	102kg
Nickname:	Wozza
Marital Status:	Engaged to Vicky
Position:	Second row
Contracted:	September 1995
Previous Clubs:	Hunslet (1993-95)
Rep. Honours:	Yorkshire under-19, Great Britain under-21

Career Highlight:	Winning the Super League
Career Ambition:	To play Test Rugby League for Great Britain
Hobbies:	Golf, swimming, computer games

SIMON JAMES KNOX

Born:	14th October 1972 at Whitehaven, Cumbria
Height:	177cm
Weight:	95kg
Nickname:	Marra
Marital Status:	Married to Paula
Position:	Second row or loose forward
Contracted:	October, 1995
Previous Clubs:	Carlisle (1991-95)
Rep. Honours:	BARLA under-19, Cumbria
Career Highlight:	Playing at Wembley
Career Ambition:	To cement my place in the Bulls team
Hobbies:	Golf, fishing, and spoiling my two-year-old son

PAUL JOHN PATRICK LOUGHLIN

Born:	28th July 1967 at St Helens
Height:	189cm
Weight:	106kg
Nickname:	Lockers
Marital Status:	Engaged to Lisa
Position:	Wing or centre
Contracted:	November, 1995
Previous Clubs:	St Helens (1984-95)
Rep. Honours:	Lancashire, Great Britain Colts, Great Britain under-21, Great Britain (including the 1988 and 1992 tours to Australia, Papua New Guinea and New Zealand)
Career Highlight:	Signing for Saints and playing the first of 16 Tests for the Lions
Career Ambition:	To win the Challenge Cup (at my sixth attempt!)
Hobbies:	Gardening, golf and darts

JAMES JOHN LOWES

Born:	11th October 1969 at Leeds
Height:	175cm
Weight:	91kg
Nickname:	Paddy
Marital Status:	Engaged to Julie

Position:	Hooker
Contracted:	February, 1996
Previous Clubs:	Leeds (1992-96), Hunslet (1986-92)
Rep. Honours:	Ireland, Great Britain (including 1996 tour to Papua New Guinea, Fiji, and New Zealand)
Career Highlight:	Captaining the Great Britain team on tour last year, winning the Man of Steel 1997
Career Ambition:	To win the Silk Cut Challenge Cup
Hobbies:	Football (esp. Leeds United), golf, reading, and drinking with the boys!

BRIAN GERRARD McDERMOTT

Born:	16th March 1970 at Wakefield
Height:	190cm
Weight:	107kg
Nickname:	Macca, Pop-eye
Marital Status:	Single
Position:	Prop
Contracted:	August, 1992
Rep. Honours:	Great Britain (including the 1996 tour of Papua New Guinea, Fiji, and New Zealand)
Career Highlight:	Playing at Wembley in the Challenge Cup
Career Ambition:	To play for Great Britain against Australia
Hobbies:	Nature studies, walking with my girlfriend, and singing on the team bus!

STEVEN SHAUN McNAMARA

Born:	18th September 1971 at Hull
Height:	180cm
Weight:	98kg
Nickname:	Macca
Marital Status:	Married to Michaela
Position:	Loose forward
Contracted:	March, 1996
Previous Clubs:	Hull (1989-96)
Rep. Honours:	Great Britain under-21, Great Britain
Career Highlight:	Playing for Great Britain
Career Ambition:	To win major trophies with the Bulls and to regain my place in the Great Britain team after missing last year's tour because of injury
Hobbies:	Golf, fishing

PAUL RICHARD MEDLEY

Born:	21st September 1966 at Leeds
Height:	183cm
Weight:	108kg
Nickname:	Medders, Bowling Ball
Marital Status:	Married to Joanne
Position:	Second row or prop
Contracted:	August, 1989
Previous Clubs:	Halifax (1989), Leeds (1984-89)
Rep. Honours:	Great Britain Colts, Great Britain under-21, Yorkshire, Great Britain (including 1988 tour to Australia, Papua New Guinea and New Zealand)
Career Highlights:	Playing in last year's Silk Cut Challenge Cup final at Wembley, winning the Super League
Career Ambition:	To play as long as Bulls club captain Graeme Bradley!
Hobbies:	Doing odd jobs around the home!

SONNY NICKLE

Born:	4th May 1970 at Leeds
Height:	185cm
Weight:	105kg
Marital Status:	Single
Position:	Second-row
Contracted:	November 1995
Previous Clubs:	St Helens (1991-95), Sheffield Eagles (1989-91), Hunslet (1987-89)
Rep. Honours:	Yorkshire colts, Great Britain under-21, Great Britain (including the 1992 tour of Papua New Guinea, Australia and New Zealand)
Career Highlight:	Winning the 1992 Premiership Final with St Helens against Wigan and making my Test debut for Great Britain
Career Ambition:	To play well every week for the Bulls and to play for Great Britain again
Hobbies:	Football (esp. Leeds United) and socialising with friends!

ROBERT ROWIRI PAUL

Born:	3rd February 1976 at Tokoroa, New Zealand
Height:	175cm
Weight:	79kg

Nickname:	Robbie
Marital Status:	Single
Position:	Scrum-half or stand-off
Contracted:	July 1994
Rep. Honours:	New Zealand
Career Highlight:	Scoring three tries, then winning the Lance Todd Trophy as man of the match, at Wembley in 1996
Career Ambition:	To captain the Bulls to victory in the Challenge Cup and become a regular in the New Zealand Test side.
Hobbies:	Painting, artwork, and listening to music

DANIEL ERIC PEACOCK

Born:	4th March 1968 at Augathella, Australia
Height:	183 cm
Weight:	90 kg
Nickname:	Bird
Marital Status:	Married to Nicole
Position:	Centre, wing or fullback
Contracted:	November, 1996
Previous Clubs:	Wests (1988-90), Gold Coast (1991-95), South Queensland (1996)
Rep. Honours:	Queensland under-19, Queensland Residents
Career Highlight:	Marking Eric Grothe in my first senior game with Wests
Career Ambition:	To win as many trophies as possible!
Hobbies:	Golf, fishing, going to the pub for a quiet one!

TAHI PIHA REIHANA

Born:	15th March 1972 at Auckland, New Zealand
Height:	180cm
Weight:	104kg
Nickname:	Ching
Marital Status:	Engaged to Victoria
Position:	Prop or second row
Contracted:	November, 1996
Previous Clubs:	Perth Reds (1995-96), South Perth (1994), Coffs Harbour (1989-93)
Rep. Honours:	Group 2, New South Wales (1991-93); North Coast, New South Wales (1991-93); Western Australia (1994)
Career Highlight:	First grade debut against the Brisbane Broncos

Career Ambition: To cement my place in the Bulls team, and to help
                     the club win major trophies
Hobbies: Surf boat racing, swimming, and dining out

JONATHAN RICHARD SCALES

Born: 28th July 1974 at Leeds
Height: 188cm
Weight: 113kg
Nickname: Scalesy
Marital Status: Single
Position: Wing
Contracted: July, 1995
Previous Clubs: Leeds (1992-95)
Rep. Honours: Called into Great Britain training squad, 1997
Career Highlight: Winning the Challenge Cup semi-finals against
                     Leeds in 1996 and 1997
Career Ambition: To win every major trophy
Hobbies: Snooker, TV viewing

STUART ARTHUR SPRUCE

Born: 3rd January 1971 at Widnes
Height: 183cm
Weight: 101kg
Nickname: Sprogger
Marital Status: Married to Caroline
Position: Fullback
Contracted: May, 1996
Previous Clubs: Widnes (1989-96)
Rep. Honours: England, Great Britain under-21, Great Britain
                     (including the 1996 tour of Papua New Guinea,
                     Fiji, and New Zealand)
Career Highlight: Winning selection for last year's Lions tour
Career Ambition: To win more major trophies with the Bulls!
Hobbies: Off-road driving, golf and football

GLEN TOMLINSON

Born: 18th March 1970 at Redcliffe, Queensland
Height: 175cm
Weight: 85kg
Nickname: Tommo
Marital Status: Single
Position: Scrum-half

Contracted:	January 1996
Previous Clubs:	Batley (1991-96), Caboolture (1987-91)
Rep. Honours:	Queensland (in cross country)
Career Highlight:	Winning the Sunshine Coast under-19 Grand Final with Caboolture and signing for the Bradford Bulls after playing at Batley
Career Ambition:	To win the Silk Cut Challenge Cup
Hobbies:	Horse racing, golf, and fishing

JEFFREY JOHN WITTENBERG

Born:	19th March 1973 at Port Macquarie, New South Wales, Australia
Height:	187cm
Weight:	112kg
Nickname:	Witto or Rusty Beef Burger
Marital Status:	Single
Position:	Prop
Contracted:	March 1997
Previous Clubs:	South Queensland Crushers (1995-96), St George (1993-94), Wynnum-Manly (1993)
Rep. Honours:	Queensland under-19, Australian under-19
Career Highlight:	Playing in the first-ever Crushers team in the Winfield Cup
Career Ambition:	To play for Australia
Hobbies:	Fishing and relaxing with friends

APPENDIX II
STONES SUPER LEAGUE

FINAL TABLE 1997

	P	W	D	L	For	Agst	Diff	PTS
Bradford Bulls	22	20	0	2	769	397	372	40
London Broncos	22	15	3	4	616	418	198	33
St Helens	22	14	1	7	592	506	86	29
Wigan Warriors	22	14	0	8	683	398	285	28
Leeds Rhinos	22	13	1	8	544	463	81	27
Salford Reds	22	11	0	11	428	495	-67	22
Halifax Blue Sox	22	8	2	12	524	549	-25	18
Sheffield Eagles	22	9	0	13	415	574	-159	18
Warrington Wolves	22	8	0	14	437	647	-210	16
Castleford Tigers	22	5	2	15	334	515	-181	12
Paris Saint-Germain	22	6	0	16	362	572	-210	12
Oldham Bears	22	4	1	17	461	631	-170	9

APPENDIX III
STONES SUPER LEAGUE

ROUND ONE
14 March, Odsal Stadium

BULLS 58
WARRINGTON WOLVES.....................20

28	Spruce
5	Scales
6	Peacock
3	Bradley
24	Loughlin
1	Paul
2	Tomlinson
22	McDermott
25	Lowes
13	Nickle
11	Donougher
23	Dwyer
26	McNamara

Subs
16	Jowitt for Donougher (64)
27	Reihana for Dwyer (2)
7	Cook for Bradley (52)
12	Medley for Nickle (29)
	Nickle for Reihana (65)

Tries: Paul (4, 25, 40), Scales (7), Spruce (42, 69), McDermott (50), McNamara (55), Lowers (75), Peacock (79)
Goals: McNamara 9

WARRINGTON: Nigel Vagana, Mateaki Mafi, Toa Kohe-Love, Jon Roper, Mark Forster, Kelly Shelford, Willie Swann, Salesi Finau, Martin Dermott, Gary Chambers, Chris Holden, Tony Tatupu, Gareth Davies. Subs: Chris Rudd, Andy Currier, Warren Stevens, George Mann.

Tries: Vagana, Rudd, Tatupu, Currier
Goals: Roper 2

Half-time: 20-8
Referee: David Campbell
Attendance: 15,017

ROUND TWO
21 March, Boundary Park

OLDHAM BEARS.....................................18
BULLS 30

28	Spruce
24	Loughlin
3	Bradley
6	Peacock
5	Scales
1	Paul
2	Tomlinson
22	McDermott
25	Lowes
13	Nickle
16	Jowitt
23	Dwyer
26	McNamara

Subs
11	Donougher for Jowitt (20)
27	Reihana for Nickle (34)
7	Cook for Scales (50)
12	Medley for McNamara (70)
	Nickle for Donougher (55)

Tries: McNamara (8), Jowitt (14), Bradley (44), Spruce (61), Nickle (79).
Goals: McNamara 4, Cook

Sin-bin: Bradley (55) - fighting

OLDHAM: Luke Goodwin, Scott Ranson, Afi Leuila, Paul Atcheson, Rob Myler, Francis Maloney, Martin Crompton, Ian Gildart, Chris McKinney, Brett Goldspink, Gary Lord, Joe Faimalo, David Bradbury. Subs: David Jones, Howard Hill, John Clarke, Paul Davidson.

Tries: Myler (2), Lord (24), Bradbury (66)
Goals Maloney 3
Sin-bin: Goodwin (55) - fighting

Half-time: 14-12
Referee: Russell Smith
Attendance: 5,604

ROUND THREE
1 April, Wheldon Road

CASTLEFORD TIGERS 38
BULLS 12

28	Spruce
7	Cook
3	Bradley
24	Loughlin
15	Christie
1	Paul
2	Tomlinson
22	McDermott
25	Lowes
17	Anderson
13	Nickle
16	Jowitt
26	McNamara

Subs
18	Knox for McNamara (32)
27	Reihana for Anderson (30)
20	Calland for Bradley (47)
10	Graham for Jowitt (55)
	Anderson For Reihana (49bb)
	Reihana for Anderson (70bb)

Tries: Paul (5, 76), Loughlin (12), Jowitt (37), McDermott (60), Lowes (68).
Goals: McNamara 3, Cook 4

CASTLEFORD: Jason Flowers, Chris Smith, Richard Gay, Adrian Flynn, Simon Middleton, Graham Steadman, Adrian Vowles, Lee Crooks, Lee St Hilaire, Dean Sampson, Lee Harland, Jason Lidden, Brendon Tuuta. Subs: David Chapman, Nathan Sykes, Paul Smith, Andrew Schick.

Tries: Flowers (29), Chapman (63)
Goals: Crooks, Vowles

Half-time: 6-18
Referee: John Connolly
Attendance: 7,882

ROUND FOUR
6 April, Odsal Stadium

BULLS 19
LONDON BRONCOS 14

28	Spruce
7	Cook
6	Peacock
3	Bradley
24	Loughlin
1	Paul
2	Tomlinson
27	Reihana
25	Lowes
17	Anderson
13	Nickle
18	Knox
26	McNamara

Subs
15	Christie for Spruce (63)
8	Wittenberg for Anderson (26)
20	Calland for Nickle (53)
12	Medley for Knox (26)
	Knox for Wittenberg (42)

Tries: Loughlin (4), Nickle (30), Cook (39)
Goals: McNamara 3
Field Goal: McNamara

LONDON: Greg Barwick, Scott Roskell, Tulsen Tollett, David Krause, Paul Smith, Adrian Spencer, Shaun Edwards, Russell Bawden, Robbie Beazley, Tony Mestrov, Matt Nable , Steve Rosolen, Terry Matterson. Subs: Josh White, Matt Salter, Peter Gill, Tony Martin.

Tries: Krause (22), Barwick (67), Nable (75)
Goal : Barwick 1

Half-time: 18 - 6
Referee: David Campbell
Attendance:15,566

ROUND FIVE
11 April, Central Park

WIGAN WARRIORS **18**
BULLS **22**

28	Spruce
7	Cook
6	Peacock
24	Loughlin
4	Ekoku
1	Paul
2	Tomlinson
27	Reihana
25	Lowes
17	Anderson
13	Nickle
23	Dwyer
3	Bradley

Subs
12	Medley for Anderson (22)
8	Wittenberg for Reihana (17)
20	Calland for Spruce (70)
18	Knox for Nickle (28)
	Anderson for Wittenberg (57)

Tries: Peacock (34, 70), Calland (74)
Goals: Cook 5

WIGAN: Jason Robinson, Darryl Cardiss, Gary Connolly, Kris Radlinski, Andy Johnson, Tony Smith, Craig Murdock, Terry O'Connor, Mick Cassidy, Stephen Holgate, Simon Haughton, Gael Tallec, Andy Farrell. Subs: David Murray, Nigel Wright, Martin Hall, Neil Baynes.

Tries: Haughton (27, 61), Smith (68)
Goals: Farrell 3

Half-time: 8-10
Referee: Stuart Cummings
Attendance: 10,710

ROUND SIX
18 April, Stade Charlety

PARIS ST GERMAIN **18**
BULLS **30**

28	Spruce
7	Cook
6	Peacock
24	Loughlin
4	Ekoku
1	Paul
2	Tomlinson
8	Wittenberg
25	Lowes
27	Reihana
23	Dwyer
3	Bradley
26	McNamara

Subs
10	Graham for Ekoku (75)
12	Medley for McNamara (24)
17	Anderson for Wittenberg (22)
18	Knox for Reihana (56)
	Wittenberg for Anderson (39,BB)
	Anderson for Wittenberg (50,BB)
	McNamara for Tomlinson (67)

Tries: Cook (16, 45), Lowes (28), Paul (73, 76)
Goals: McNamara 4, Cook

PSG: Fabien Devecchi, Anthony Wall, Jamie Olejnik, Deon Bird, Phil Bergman, Jeremy Robinson, Matthew O'Connor, Joe Taylor, David O'Donnell, Tony Priddle, Wayne Sing, Michael Hogue, David Lomax. Subs: Troy Bellamy, James Durkin, Nick Hyde, Adam Peters

Tries: Olejnik (32, 39), Robinson (57), Bird (65)
Goal: Wall

Half-time: 8-14
Referee: John Connolly
Att: 9,745

ROUND SEVEN
23 April, Odsal Stadium

ROUND EIGHT
27 April, Odsal Stadium

BULLS 28
HALIFAX BLUE SOX 26

BULLS 54
SHEFFIELD EAGLES 10

7	Cook
4	Ekoku
20	Calland
24	Loughlin
5	Scales
3	Bradley
2	Tomlinson
17	Anderson
15	Lowes
27	Reihana
18	Knox
23	Dwyer
26	McNamara

Subs
14   Forshaw not used
8   Wittenberg for Anderson (32)
6   Peacock for Loughlin (35)
10   Graham for Tomlinson 29)
     Anderson for Reihana (66)

Tries: Knox (2,44,61), Calland (20),
McNamara (57)
Goals: McNamara 4

28	Spruce
7	Cook
6	Peacock
24	Loughilin
4	Ekoku
3	Bradley
2	Tomlinson
22	McDermott
25	Lowes
17	Anderson
13	Nickle
18	Knox
26	McNamara

Subs
15   Christie for Cook (66)
12   Medley for Knox (22)
10   Graham for Bradley (61)
8   Wittenberg for Anderson (51)
     Knox for Wittenberg 51)
     Anderson for Medley (59)

Tries: Ekoku (2, 15), Bradley (34, 61),
Peacock (40), Nickle (47), Anderson (63, 65),
McNamara (73), McDermott (80)
Goals: McNamara 7

HALIFAX: Mike Umaga, Asa Amone, Martin Moana, Martin Pearson, Damian Munro, Chris Chester, Wayne Parker, Karl Harrison, Paul Rowley, Kelvin Skerrett, Michael Jackson, Carl Gillespie, Simon Baldwin. Subs: Craig Dean, Paul Highton, David Bouveng, Wayne Jackson.

Tries: Munro (14), Pearson (28,67), Moana (54), Chester (71)
Goals: Pearson 3

SHEFFIELD: Lynton Stott, Waisale Sovatabua, Willie Morganson, Wheta Taewa, Jean-Marc Garcia, David Mycoe, Mark Aston, Paul Broadbent, Jason Erba, Steve Edmed, Danny McAllister, Andy Hay, Rod Doyle. Subs: Wayne Flynn, Paul Dixon, Alex Thompson, Lawrence Taylor.

Try: Mycoe (18)
Goals: Aston 3

Half-time: 12-10
Referee: David Campbell
Attendance: 13,285

Half-time: 20-10
Referee: Steve Presley
Attendance: 14,834

ROUND NINE
11 May, Odsal Stadium

BULLS 38
ST HELENS 18

28	Spruce
5	Scales
24	Loughlin
6	Peacock
4	Ekoku
3	Bradley
2	Tomlinson
22	McDermott
25	Lowes
27	Reihana
14	Forshaw
23	Dwyer
26	McNamara
Subs	
10	Graham for Bradley (59)
20	Calland for Ekoku (35)
17	Anderson for Reihana (20)
18	Knox for Dwyer (46)
	Reihana for Anderson (68)

Tries: Dwyer (9), Forshaw (21,45), McNamara (33), Loughlin (49), Knox (79)
Goals: McNamara 7

ST HELENS: Steve Prescott, Danny Arnold, Andy Haigh, Paul Newlove, Anthony Sullivan, Tommy Martyn, Bobbie Goulding, Apollo Perelini, Keiron Cunningham, Julian O'Neill, Chris Morley, Derek McVey, Karle Hammond. Subs: Ian Pickavance, Vila Matautia, Chris Joynt, Andy Northey.

Tries: Sullivan (16), Perelini (63), Martyn (penalty try, 76)
Goals: Goulding 3

Half-time: 20-6
Referee: Russell Smith
Attendance: 18,387

ROUND TEN
18 May, Wilderspool

WARRINGTON WOLVES..........................14
BULLS 38

28	Spruce
4	Ekoku
20	Calland
6	Peacock
5	Scales
3	Bradley
2	Tomlinson
17	Anderson
25	Lowes
27	Reihana
12	Medley
14	Forshaw
26	McNamara
Subs	
10	Graham for Medley (24)
22	McDermott for Anderson (24)
8	Wittenberg for Reihana (35)
24	Loughlin for Spruce (55)
	Spruce for Peacock (59)
	Reihana for Wittenberg (75)

Tries: Calland (3), Anderson (15), Forshaw (27), Lowes (37), Peacock (52), Tomlinson (55, 77).
Goals: McNamara 5

WARRINGTON: Chris Rudd, Richard Henare, Paul Wingfield, Nigel Vagana, Mark Forster, Kelly Shelford, Lee Briers, Warren Stevens, John Hough, George Mann, Paul Hulme, Tony Tatupu, Paul Sculthorpe. Subs: Tony Thorniley, Salesi Finau, Ian Knott, Shaun Geritas.

Tries: Wingfield (50), Briers (59), Knott (66)
Goals: Briers

Half-time: 0-22
Referee: Robert Connolly
Attendance: 7,043

ROUND ELEVEN
23 May, Odsal Stadium

BULLS 42
OLDHAM BEARS 28

28	Spruce
4	Ekoku
20	Calland
24	Loughlin
5	Scales
6	Peacock
2	Tomlinson
22	McDermott
25	Lowes
27	Reihana
14	Forshaw
12	Medley
26	McNamara

Subs
10	Graham for Reihana (31)
18	Knox for Medley (26)
17	Anderson for Lowes (31)
8	Wittenberg for Forshaw (61)
	Lowes for Spruce (68)
	Reihana for Anderson (75)

Tries: Ekoku (4, 48), Scales (11, 61), Spruce (46), Tomlinson (51, 57), Wittenberg (76)
Goals: McNamara 5

OLDHAM: Paul Atcheson, Scott Ranson, Darren Abram, Rob Myler, David Jones, Francis Maloney, Martin Crompton, Gary Lord, John Clarke, Tony Nuttall, Joe Faimalo, Paul Davidson, Paul Topping. Subs: Jimmy Cowan, Brett Goldspink, Howard Hill, David Stephenson.

Tries: Faimalo (19), Maloney (21), Davidson (30, 70), Myler (67)
Goals: Maloney 3, Topping 1

Half-time: 10-18
Referee: Steve Ganson
Attendance: 13,262

ROUND TWELVE
27 May, Thrum Hall

HALIFAX BLUE SOX 26
BULLS...30

28	Spruce
24	Loughlin
20	Calland
6	Peacock
5	Scales
3	Bradley
2	Tomlinson
8	Wittenberg
25	Lowes
17	Anderson
14	Forshaw
18	Knox
26	McNamara

Subs
22	McDermott for Wittenberg (10)
10	Graham for McNamara (45)
12	Medley for Knox (14)
27	Reihana for Anderson (48)
	Knox for Medley (55)

Tries: McDermott (30), Knox (58), Spruce (62, 64), Scales (70), Loughlin (73)
Goals: McNamara, Loughlin 2

HALIFAX: Mike Umaga, Fereti Tuilagi, Daio Powell, Dave Bouveng, Asa Amone, Martin Pearson, Craig Dean, Karl Harrison, Chris Chester, Wayne Jackson, Paul Highton, Carl Gillespie, Martin Moana. Subs: Damian Munro, Richard Marshall, Michael Slicker, Danny Seal.

Tries: Dean (2), Gillespie (9, 23), Amone (18, 40)
Goals: Pearson 3

Half-time: 26-6
Referee: David Campbell
Attendance: 6,252

ROUND THIRTEEN
1 June, The Willows

SALFORD REDS..24
BULLS 40

28	Spruce
20	Calland
24	Loughlin
6	Peacock
5	Scales
3	Bradley
2	Tomlinson
17	Anderson
25	Lowes
22	McDermott
14	Forshaw
18	Knox
26	McNamara

Subs
8	Wittenberg for McDermott (27)
10	Graham for Lowes (48)
12	Medley for Knox (48)
27	Reihana for Anderson (24)
	Anderson for Reihana (70)

Tries: Tomlinson (10), Bradley (20,28),
Wittenberg (40), Lowes (41), Forshaw (55),
Calland (58)
Goals: McNamara 6

SALFORD: Gary Broadbent, Fata Sini, Darren Rogers, Nathan McAvoy, Phil Coussons, Steve Blakeley, Ian Watson, Paul Southern, Peter Edwards, Cliff Eccles, Esene Faimalo, Lokeni Savelio, David Hulme. Subs: Richard Smith, Andy Platt, Andy Burgess, Scott Martin.

Tries: Faimalo (9), Watson (44), Martin (52), McAvoy (67), Smith (79)
Goals: Blakeley, Watson

Half-time: 4-24
Referee: Stuart Cummings
Attendance: 8,241

ROUND FOURTEEN
29 June, Headingley

LEEDS RHINOS 16
BULLS 32

28	Spruce
30	Hodgson
6	Peacock
3	Bradley
20	Calland
1	Paul
2	Tomlinson
22	McDermott
25	Lowes
17	Anderson
14	Forshaw
23	Dwyer
26	McNamara

Subs
8	Wittenberg for McDermott (76)
10	Graham for Paul (55)
13	Nickle for Forshaw (30)
27	Reihana for Anderson (22)
	Forshaw for Dwyer (50)
	Anderson for Reihana (66)

Tries: Bradley (3), McNamara (24), Nickle (47), Graham (55), Hodgson (76)
Goals: McNamara 6

LEEDS: Damian Gibson, Paul Sterling, Francis Cummins, Phil Hassan, Marcus St Hilaire, Iestyn Harris, Ryan Sheridan, Martin Masella, Wayne Collins, Barrie McDermott, Adrian Morley, Anthony Farrell, Gary Mercer. Subs: Graham Holroyd, Jamie Mathiou, Terry Newton, Andy Hay.

Tries: McDermott (11), Mercer (63)
Goals: Harris 4

Half-time: 10-12
Referee: Russell Smith
Attendance: 19,137

ROUND FIFTEEN
2 July, Odsal Stadium

BULLS 34
CASTLEFORD TIGERS 20

28	Spruce
30	Hodgson
24	Loughlin
20	Calland
5	Scales
10	Graham
2	Tomlinson
8	Wittenberg
25	Lowes
12	Medley
13	Nickle
14	Forshaw
26	McNamara
Subs	
3	Bradley (not used)
27	Reihana for Wittenberg (30)
17	Anderson for Medley (20)
18	Knox for Nickle (50)
	Nickle for Knox (72)

Tries: Tomlinson (35, 50), Scales (73, 75),
Graham (57), McNamara (54)
Goals: McNamara 5

CASTLEFORD: Jason Flowers, Richard Gay, David
Chapman, Adrian Vowles, Chris Smith, Brad Davis, Mike
Ford, Dean Sampson, Richard Russell, Richard McKell,
Andrew Schick, Jason Lidden, Brendon Tuuta. Subs:
Nathan Sykes, Danny Orr, Grant Anderson, Graham
Steadman.

Tries: Vowles (62, 66), Chapman (70), Flowers (14)
Goals: Davis, Orr

Dismissal: Sampson (80) - fighting

Half-time: 4-6
Referee: David Campbell
Attendance: 11,873

ROUND SIXTEEN
6 July, Knowsley Road

ST HELENS...20
BULLS 38

28	Spruce
20	Calland
6	Peacock
24	Loughlin
30	Hodgson
3	Bradley
2	Tomlinson
22	McDermott
25	Lowes
27	Reihana
14	Forshaw
23	Dwyer
26	McNamara
Subs	
10	Graham for Spruce (77)
13	Nickle for Dwyer (35)
16	Jowitt not used
17	Anderson for Reihana (21)
	Dwyer for Anderson (54)
	Reihana for Forshaw (68)

Tries: Lowes (3, 39), Hodgson (23), Calland
(27, 45), Peacock (61), Bradley (65)
Goals: McNamara 5

SAINTS: Andy Haigh, Danny Arnold, Alan Hunte, Paul
Newlove, Anthony Sullivan, Sean Long, Scott Barrow,
Andy Leathem, Keiron Cunningham, Julian O'Neill,
Chris Joynt, Vila Matautia, Karle Hammond. Subs: Joey
Hayes, Ian Pickavance, Chris Morley, Paul Anderson.

Tries: Long (7), Arnold (35, 69), Hayes (77)
Goals: Long 2

Half-time: 8-20
Referee: Stuart Cummings
Attendance: 10,277

ROUND SEVENTEEN
13 July, Odsal Stadium

BULLS 34
SALFORD REDS............................14

28	Spruce
20	Calland
24	Loughlin
3	Bradley
30	Hodgson
10	Graham
2	Tomlinson
22	McDermott
25	Lowes
8	Wittenberg
13	Nickle
23	Dwyer
26	McNamara

Subs
14 Forshaw for Dwyer (25)
27 Reihana for Wittenberg (25)
16 Jowitt for Graham (63)
9 Crouthers for Nickle (70)
    Wittenberg for McDermott (35)
    McDermott for Reihana (57)

Tries: Graham (12), Dwyer (37), Lowes (53),
Hodgson (60), Calland (70), McDermott (80)
Goals: McNamara 2, Loughlin 3

Sin-bin: Wittenberg (52) for fighting

SALFORD: Gary Broadbent, Fata Sini, Nathan McAvoy,
Scott Martin, Darren Rogers, Steve Blakeley, Ian Watson,
Andy Platt, Peter Edwards, Cliff Eccles, Lukeni Savelio,
Esene Faimalo, Craig Randall. Subs: Paul Forber, Paul
Southern, Andy Burgess, Mark Lee

Tries: Rogers (5), Sini (74)
Goals: Blakeley 3

Sin-bin: Edwards (52) for fighting

Half-time: 16-10
Referee: Steve Presley
Attendance: 14,095

ROUND EIGHTEEN
10 August, Odsal Stadium

BULL..22
LEEDS RHINOS 8

28	Spruce
10	Graham
24	Loughlin
6	Peacock
5	Scales
3	Bradley
1	Paul
22	McDermott
25	Lowes
27	Reihana
23	Dwyer
14	Forshaw
26	McNamara

Subs
17 Anderson for Reihana (21)
8 Wittenberg for Lowes (73)
11 Donougher for Dwyer (36)
2 Tomlinson for Paul (45)
    Dwyer for Forshaw (40)
    Reihana for Anderson (50)
    Forshaw for Donougher (56)

Tries: Scales (11), Paul (12, 26), Lowes (60)
Goals: McNamara 3

Sin-Bin: Lowes (31) - fighting

LEEDS: Damian Gibson, Paul Sterling, Phil Hassan,
Richie Blackmore, Marvin Golden, Iestyn Harris, Gavin
Brown, Martin Masella, Wayne Collins, Jamie Mathiou,
Adrian Morley, Terry Newton, Gary Mercer. Subs:
Graham Holroyd, Francis Cummins, Andy Hay, Anthony
Farrell.

Tries: Golden (47)
Goals: Harris 2

Sin-bin: Wayne Collins (31) - fighting
On report: Anthony Farrell (67) - kicking, Gary Mercer
(76) - high, late tackle

Half-time: 14-2
Referee: Russell Smith
Attendance: 16,542

ROUND NINETEEN
17 August, Don Valley Stadium

SHEFFIELD EAGLES 12
BULLS 32

28	Spruce
4	Ekoku
6	Peacock
24	Loughlin
5	Scales
3	Bradley
1	Paul
22	McDermott
25	Lowes
8	Wittenberg
13	Nickle
11	Donougher
26	McNamara
Sub	
27	Reihana for Wittenberg (29)
14	Forshaw for Donougher (2-bb)
23	Dwyer for Nickle (20)
2	Tomlinson for Lowes (1-bb)

Tries: Peacock (17), Dwyer (44), Wittenberg (71), Lowes (75), Forshaw (79)
Goals: McNamara 6

Sin-bin: Spruce (52) holding down

ROUND TWENTY
22 August, Odsal Stadium

BULLS 68
PARIS ST GERMAIN 0

30	Hodgson
15	Christie
24	Loughlin
6	Peacock
9	Crouthers
1	Paul
2	Tomlinson
17	Anderson
25	Lowes
8	Wittenberg
11	Donougher
13	Nickle
26	McNamara
Subs	
12	Medley for Anderson (25)
10	Graham for Lowes (48-bb)
16	Jowitt for Medley (48)
28	Spruce for Hodgson (16)
	Lowes for Graham (55-bb)
	Graham for Donougher (58)
	Medley for Paul (64)
	Anderson for Nickle (69)

Tries: Loughlin (2), Hodgson (4), Tomlinson (9), Wittenberg (20), Peacock (42, 51, 68), Lowes (47, 64), Spruce (49), Christie (55), Crouthers (57), Medley (67, 78)
Goals: McNamara 6

SHEFFIELD: Waisale Sovatabua, Nick Pinkney, Willie Morganson, Whetu Taewa, Matt Crowther, David Mycoe, Mark Aston, Paul Broadbent, Marcus Vassilakopoulos, Alex Thompson, Keith Senior, Danny McAllister, Rod Doyle. Subs: Ricky Wright, Jason Erba, Dale Laughton, Jean-Marc Garcia.

Tries: Taewa (33), McAllister (39)
Goals: Aston 2

PSG: Nick Hoyle, Sean Mahony, Jason Eade, Phillipe Ricard, Nick Couttet, Fabien Devecchi, Alex Couttet, Tony Priddle, Troy Bellamy, Didier Cabestany, Anthony Hancock, Michael Hogue, Pascal Jampy. Subs: Romain Sort, Jerome Azema, Abderazak Elkhalouki, Frederic Teixido.

Half-time: 10-4
Referee: Steve Ganson
Attendance: 10,500

Half-time: 20-0
Referee: John Connolly
Attendance: 17,128

ROUND TWENTY-ONE
25 August, Odsal Stadium

BULLS 18
WIGAN WARRIORS 33

28	Spruce
4	Ekoku
20	Calland
6	Peacock
5	Scales
3	Bradley
2	Tomlinson
22	McDermott
25	Lowes
8	Wittenberg
23	Dwyer
14	Forshaw
26	McNamara

Subs
1	Paul for Scales (22)
17	Anderson for Wittenberg (26)
18	Knox for Calland (72)
10	Graham for Lowes (22 bb)
	Lowes for Graham (40bb)
	Graham for Dwyer (58)
	Scales for Paul (69)
	Wittenberg for Anderson (62)

Tries: Scales (1), Lowes (21), Dwyer (35)
Goals: McNamara (3)
Sin-bin: James Lowes (69) for dissent

ROUND TWENTY-TWO
31 August, The Stoop

LONDON BRONCOS 28
BULLS 24

28	Spruce
24	Loughlin
6	Peacock
3	Bradley
5	Scales
1	Paul
2	Tomlinson
22	McDermott
25	Lowes
8	Wittenberg
13	Nickle
14	Forshaw
26	McNamara

Subs
23	Dwyer for Wittenberg (23)
11	Donougher for Reihana (23)
27	Reihana for Nickle (57)
4	Ekoku (not used)
	Wittenberg for McDermott (64)
	McDermott for Donougher (68)

Tries: Bradley (5), Spruce (25), Dwyer (29), Loughlin (57)
Goals: McNamara 4

WIGAN: Jason Robinson, Danny Ellison, Gary Connolly, Kris Radlinski, Andy Johnson, Henry Paul, Craig Murdock, Lee Hansen, Martin Hall, Neil Cowie, Simon Haughton, Mick Cassidy, Andy Farrell. Subs: Stephen Holgate, Gael Tallec, Paul Johnson, Jon Clarke.

Tries: Robinson (37, 57), Paul (54), Connolly (63), Cowie (76) Goals: Farrell (6) Field-goal: Farrell

LONDON: Nick Mardon, Butch Fatnowna, Tony Martin, Greg Barwick, Martin Offiah, Tulsen Tollett, Shaun Edwards, Tony Mestrov, Robbie Beazley, Kim Howard, Matt Dunford, Russell Bawden, Terry Matterson. Subs: Matt Salter, Kerrod Toby, Scott Roskell, Andrew Hamilton.

Tries: Edwards (14), Offiah (18, 76), Bawden (34), Beazley (45), Martin (62)
Goals: Barwick 2

Half-time: 18-6
Referee: Steve Presley
Attendance: 16,761

Half-time:14-18
Referee: John Connolly
Attendance: 9,166

APPENDIX IV
SILK CUT CHALLENGE CUP

ROUND FOUR (exempt from previous three rounds)
9 February

ROUND FIVE
22 February

HUNSLET HAWKS..................................10
BULLS 62

LONDON BRONCOS 12
BULLS 34

10	Graham
7	Cook
6	Peacock
24	Loughlin
5	Scales
3	Bradley
2	Tomlinson
22	McDermott
25	Lowes
23	Dwyer
11	Donougher
13	Nickle
26	McNamara
Subs	
28	Spruce for Graham (52)
1	Paul for McNamara (52)
16	Jowitt for Dwyer (49)
18	Knox for Donougher (40)

28	Spruce
5	Scales
3	Bradley
6	Peacock
24	Loughlin
1	Paul
2	Tomlinson
22	McDermott
25	Lowes
27	Reihana
11	Donougher
13	Nickle
26	McNamara
Subs	
12	Medley for Reihana (22)
18	Knox for McNamara (39)
16	Jowitt for Medley (47)
7	Cook for Spruce (53)
	McNamara for Knox (40)
	Reihana for McDermott (64)

Tries: Peacock (6, 21), Donougher (13, 25), Nickle (18), Cook (32, 62), Loughlin (38, 76), McDermott (71), Jowitt (80)
Goals: McNamara 6, Cook 3

Sin-bins: Bradley (55) - dissent, Tomlinson (67) - fighting

Tries: Loughlin (2), Nickle (37, 47), Paul (65), Tomlinson (74), Cook (79)
Goals: McNamara 5

HUNSLET: Lee Senior, Richard Baker, Craig Booth, Mick Coult, Gary Richardson, Paul Mansson, David Brook, Nicky Rushton, Graham Southernwood, Simon Tuffs, Neil Bradbrook, Stuart Flowers, Gareth Cochrane. Subs: Steve Pryce, Brendan Hill, Chris Ross, Jimmy Walker.

Tries: Southernwood (45), Flowers (46)
Goals: Booth. Sin-bin: Brook (67) - fighting

BRONCOS: Tony Martin, Mark Maguire, Paul Smith, David Krause, Scott Roskell, Tulsen Tollett, Josh White, Tony Mestrov, Robbie Beazley, Russell Bawden, Steve Rosolen, Peter Gill, Terry Matterson. Subs: Greg Barwick, Matt Dunford, Roger Best, Adrian Spencer.

Tries: Roskell (51), Krause (59)
Goals: Barwick 2

Half-time: 0-40
Referee: Karl Kirkpatrick
Attendance: 6,102

Half-time: 2-10
Referee: David Campbell
Attendance: 6,102

229

QUARTER FINAL
9 March

OLDHAM BEARS 12
BULLS 38

28	Spruce
5	Scales
3	Bradley
6	Peacock
24	Loughlin
1	Paul
2	Tomlinson
22	McDermott
25	Lowes
27	Reihana
11	Donougher
23	Dwyer
26	McNamara

Subs
12 Medley for Reihana (39)
13 Nickle for Dwyer (48)
16 Jowitt for McDermott (60)
7 Cook for Peacock (60)
Peacock for Spruce (73)
McDermott for Donougher (73)

Tries: Loughlin (3), Spruce (16), Peacock (32), Paul (48), Tomlinson (55, 59)
Goals: McNamara 7

OLDHAM: Paul Atcheson, Scott Ranson, Darren Abram, Vince Fawcett, Rob Myler, Francis Maloney, Martin Crompton, Ian Gildart, Chris McKinney, Brett Goldspink, Gary Lord, David Bradbury, Howard Hill. Subs: John Clarke, Paul Davidson, Joe Faimalo, Luke Goodwin.

Tries: Abram (22), Faimalo (62)
Goals: Maloney 2

Half-time: 6-18
Referee: Stuart Cummings (Widnes)
Attendance: 11,284

SEMI FINAL (at McAlpine Stadium, Huddersfield)
29 March

BULLS 24
LEEDS RHINOS 10

28	Spruce
5	Scales
6	Peacock
24	Loughlin
7	Cook
3	Bradley
1	Paul
22	McDermott
25	Lowes
27	Reihana
13	Nickle
23	Dwyer
26	McNamara

Subs:
2 Tomlinson for McNamara (56)
20 Calland for Peacock (37)
12 Medley for Reihana (4)
16 Jowitt for Dwyer (32bb)
Dwyer for Jowitt (44bb)
Reihana for Medley (48)
Medley for Dwyer (66bb)
Jowitt for Nickle (71bb)

Tries: Lowes (28), Loughlin (39), McNamara (43), Medley (69)
Goals: McNamara 3, Cook 1
Dismissal: McDermott for punching (75)
Sinbin: Nickle for fighting (33)

RHINOS: Damian Gibson, Paul Sterling, Richard Blackmore, Francis Cummins, Phil Hassan, Tony Kemp, Graham Holroyd, Martin Masella, Wayne Collins, Jamie Mathiou, Adrian Morley, Anthony Farrell, Gary Mercer. Subs: Leroy Rivett, Ryan Sheridan, Terry Newton, Barrie McDermott.

Tries: Kemp (6), Masella (55)
Goal: Holroyd 1
Sinbin: Hassan for fighting (33), Blackmore for play the ball offence (38)

Half-time: 10-4
Referee: Russell Smith (Castleford)
Attendance: 18,193

FINAL (at Wembley Stadium)
3 May

ST HELENS 32
BULLS 22

28	Spruce
4	Ekoku
6	Peacock
24	Loughlin
7	Cook
3	Bradley
1	Paul
22	McDermott
25	Lowes
27	Reihana
13	Nickle
23	Dwyer
26	McNamara

Subs
12 Medley for Reihana (27bb)
20 Calland for Loughlin (39)
2 Tomlinson for Paul (47)
18 Knox for Dwyer (64)
   Reihana for Medley (40)
   Paul for Cook (59)
   Medley for Reihana (64)
   Dwyer for Medley (71)

Tries: Peacock (11), Loughlin (19),
Tomlinson (63), Lowes (77)
Goals: McNamara 3

SAINTS: Steve Prescott, Danny Arnold, Andy Haigh,
Paul Newlove, Anthony Sullivan, Tommy Martyn,
Bobbie Goulding, Apollo Perelini, Keiron Cunningham,
Julian O'Neill, Chris Joynt, Derek McVey, Karle
Hammond. Subs: Ian Pickavance, Vila Matautia, Andy
Northey, Chris Morley.

Tries: Martyn (8, 27), Hammond (39), Joynt (48),
Sullivan (52)
Goals: Goulding 6

Half-time: 10-16
Referee: Stuart Cummings (Widnes)
Attendance: 78,022 (capacity)

APPENDIX V
WORLD CLUB CHAMPIONSHIP

GAME ONE
9 June, Odsal Stadium

BULLS 16
PENRITH...20

28	Spruce
20	Calland
6	Peacock
24	Loughlin
5	Scales
1	Paul
2	Tomlinson
27	Reihana
25	Lowes
22	McDermott
14	Forshaw
26	McNamara
3	Bradley

Subs
8	Wittenberg for Anderson (46)
10	Graham for Knox (75)
18	Knox for Paul (47)
17	Anderson for Reihana (16)
	Reihana for McDermott (49)
	Paul for Spruce (57)

Tries: Scales (12), Peacock (25), Spruce (39)
Goals: McNamara 2

PANTHERS: Peter Jorgensen, Robbie Beckett, Sid Domic, Ryan Girdler, Jason Williams, Steve Carter, Craig Gower, Phil Adamson, Danny Farrar, Carl McNamara, Matt Adamson, Jody Gall, Darren Brown. Subs: Brad Drew, Brett Boyd, Bobbie Thompson, David Alexander.

Tries: Jorgensen (15), Girdler (49), Brown (69), Domic (78) Goals: Girdler 2
On Report: Matt Adamson - high tackle

Half-time: 16-6
Referee: David Campbell
Attendance: 14,378

GAME TWO
14 June, Odsal Stadium

BULLS 16
AUCKLAND WARRIORS 20

6	Peacock
20	Calland
24	Loughlin
3	Bradley
30	Hodgson
1	Paul
2	Tomlinson
27	Reihana
25	Lowes
22	McDermott
14	Forshaw
12	Medley
26	McNamara

Subs
8	Wittenberg for McDermott (54)
10	Graham for Medley (27)
18	Knox for Medley (68)
17	Anderson for Reihana (27)
	Medley for Paul (49)
	Paul for Anderson (78)

Tries: Bradley (42), Forshaw (58)
Goals: McNamara 3, Loughlin

Sin-bin: McNamara (50) - professional foul

AUCKLAND: Matthew Ridge, Sean Hoppe, Tea Ropati, Shane Endacott, Paul Staladi, Gene Ngamu, Stacey Jones, Joe Vagana, Syd Eru, Brady Malam, Tony Tuimavave, Stephen Kearney, Denis Betts. Subs: Mark Horo, Bryan Henare, Logan Swann, Meti Noovao

Tries: Jones (3), Ridge (51), Staladi (74) Goals: Ridge 4
Dismissal: Syd Eru (37) - high tackle

Half-time: 2-8
Referee: Russell Smith
Attendance: 13,133

THE WORLD CLUB CHAMPIONSHIP GAMES

GAME THREE
20 June, Odsal Stadium

BULLS 10
CRONULLA SARKS 30

28	Spruce
30	Hodgson
20	Calland
6	Peacock
24	Loughlin
3	Bradley
2	Tomlinson
27	Reihana
25	Lowes
22	McDermott
14	Forshaw
23	Dwyer
26	McNamara

Subs
13 Nickle for Forshaw (32)
10 Graham for McNamara (49)
12 Medley for McDermott (52)
17 Anderson for Reihana (23-bb)
   Forshaw for Nickle (61)
   Nickle for Dwyer (70)
   Anderson for Medley (65)

Tries: Loughlin (3), Nickle (79)
Goals: Loughlin

Sin Bin: Bradley (29) - dissent, Tomlinson
(56) - holding down

CRONULLA: David Peachey, Mat Rogers, Andrew
Ettingshausen, Russell Richardson, Richard Barnett,
Mitch Healey, Paul Green, Danny Lee, Dean Treister,
Jason Stevens, Wade Forrester, Nick Graham, Tawera
Nikau. Subs: Adam Dykes, Martin Lang, Geoff Bell, Tiaan
Strauss.

Tries: Rogers (11, 42, 51), Strauss (31)
Goals: Rogers 7

Sin-bin: Graham (78) - obstruction

Half-time: 4-16
Referee: Stuart Cummings
Attendance: 10,756

GAME FOUR
19 July, Ericsson Stadium

AUCKLAND WARRIORS 64
BULLS 14

28	Spruce
20	Calland
6	Peacock
24	Loughlin
30	Hodgson
3	Bradley (c)
2	Tomlinson
27	Reihana
25	Lowes
22	McDermott
23	Dwyer
13	Nickle
26	McNamara

Subs
17 Anderson
14 Forshaw
10 Graham
8 Wittenberg

Tries: Bradley (7), Lowes (22), McDermott
(73)
Goal: Loughlin

AUCKLAND: Marc Ellis, Sean Hoppe, Tea Ropati,
Anthony Swann, Lee Oudenryn, Gene Ngamu, Stacey
Jones, Joe Vagana, Syd Eru, Brady Malam, Awen
Guttenbeil, Steve Kearney, Logan Swann. Subs: Mark
Horo, Bryan Henare, Denis Betts, Shane Endacott

Tries: Oudenryn (3), Eru (16), Hoppe (30, 59), Betts (42),
Ellis (45), Ropati (53, 62, 77), Ngamu (57)
Goals: Ngamu 12

Halftime: 24-8
Referee: Bill Harrigan
Attendance: 13,000

GAME FIVE
28 July, Panthers Stadium

PENRITH PANTHERS 54
BULLS 14

28	Spruce
20	Calland
6	Peacock
3	Bradley
30	Hodgson
1	Paul
2	Tomlinson
22	McDermott
25	Lowes
27	Reihana
23	Dwyer
14	Forshaw
13	Nickle

Subs
17 Anderson for McDermott (24)
10 Graham for Hodgson (55)
9   Crouthers for Paul (73)
16 Jowett for Reihana (33)
    Reihana for Jowett (48)
    McDermott for Anderson (52)

Tries: Forshaw (15), Peacock (58), Calland (70)
Goals: Hodgson

Sinbin: Lowes (38) - striking an opponent, Calland (39) - dissent
On report: Nickle (47) suspected high tackle on Domic

PENRITH: Peter Jorgensen, Andrew Hinson, Bobby Thompson, Sid Domic, Jason Williams, Ryan Girdler, Craig Gower, Phil Adamson, Danny Farrar, Carl McNamara, Matt Adamson, Tony Puletua, Jody Gall. Subs: Brett Boyd, Darren Brown, Chris Hicks, Gordon Falcon.

Tries: Girdler (5, 75), Jorgensen (32), Gower (40), Farrar (45), Thompson (48), Hinson (51), M Adamson (62), Brown (68),
Goals: Girdler 9

Half-time: 22-6
Referee: Bill Harrigan
Attendance: 5,336

GAME SIX
3 August, Shark Park

CRONULLA SHARKS 40
BULLS...12

28	Spruce
20	Calland
6	Peacock
3	Bradley
10	Graham
1	Paul
2	Tomlinson
22	McDermott
23	Dwyer
27	Reihana
11	Donougher
14	Forshaw
26	McNamara

Subs
24 Loughlin for Peacock (18)
16 Jowitt for Donougher (23)
8   Wittenberg for Reihana (34)
18 Knox for Paul (72)
    Donougher for Jowitt (53)
    Peacock for Calland (59)

Tries: Bradley (50, 60)
Goals: McNamara 2

CRONULLA: Brett Howland, Mat Rogers, Andrew Ettingshausen, Russell Richardson, Geoff Bell, Mitch Healey, Paul Green, Jason Stevens, Adam Dykes, Danny Lee, Chris McKenna, Les Davidson, Tawera Nikau. Subs: Martin Lang, Craig Greenhill, Sean Ryan, Wade Forrester.

Tries: McKenna (3), Howland (10), Nikau (23), Ettingshausen (27), Dykes (65), Richardson (71), Rogers (74)
Goals: Rogers 6

Half-time: 24-0
Referee: Brian Grant
Attendances: 8,272

QUARTERFINAL
3 October, Ericsson Stadium

AUCKLAND WARRIORS..........................**62**
BULLS **14**

28	Spruce
5	Scales
6	Peacock
9	Crouthers
4	Ekoku
3	Bradley
1	Paul
17	Anderson
10	Graham
22	McDermott
14	Forshaw
13	Nickle
26	McNamara
Subs	
12	Medley
27	Reihana
8	Wittenberg
11	Donougher

Tries: Ekoku (32), Bradley (35)
Goals: McNamara 3

AUCKLAND: Matthew Ridge, Sean Hoppe, Anthony Swann, Shane Endacott, Lee Oudenryn, Gene Ngamu, Stacey Jones, Joe Vagana, Syd Eru, Brady Malam, Denis Betts, Steve Kearney, Logan Swann. Subs: Mark Ellis, Mark Horo, Awen Guttenbeil, Tony Tuimavave.

Tries: Jones (19), Ngamu (23), Hoppe (29, 66), L Swann (52), Eru (57), Ridge (59, 73), Ellis (69), A Swann (79)
Goals: Ridge 9

Half Time: 20-14
Referee: Bill Harrigan
Att: 12,084

APPENDIX VI
PREMIERSHIP / OTHER GAMES

PREMIERSHIP QUARTERFINAL
14 September, Odsal Stadium

BULLS..12
CASTLEFORD TIGERS 25

28	Spruce
20	Calland
24	Loughlin
6	Peacock
4	Ekoku
1	Paul
2	Tomlinson
22	McDermott
25	Lowes
27	Reihana
14	Forshaw
23	Dwyer
26	McNamara

Subs
13	Nickle for McNamara (35)
8	Wittenberg for Reihana (22)
10	Graham for Loughlin (58)
16	Jowitt for Wittenberg (51)
	McNamara for McDermott (60)
	McDermott for Lowes (75)

Tries: Lowes (38), Forshaw (60)
Goals: McNamara, Loughlin

Dismissal: Matt Calland (12) - punching
Sin-bin: Danny Peacock (42) - fighting

CASTLEFORD: Jason Flowers, Richard Gay, Adrian Vowles, Jason Critchley, Chris Smith, Brad Davis, Mike Ford, Richard McKell, Richard Russell, Nathan Sykes, Andrew Schick, Jason Lidden, Brendon Tuuta. Subs: Danny Orr, Graham Steadman, Ian Tonks, Lee Harland

Tries: Tuuta (15), Critchley (28), Smith (50), Davis (79)
Goals: Davis 3, Steadman Field-goal: Ford
Sin-bin: Chris Smith (12) - fighting, Adrian Vowles (42) - fighting

Half-time: 8-11
Referee: Robert Connolly
Attendance: 10,300

JOE PHILLIPS MEMORIAL TROPHY
2 February, Odsal Stadium

BULLS 36
KEIGHLEY COUGARS 20

10	Graham
7	Cook
6	Peacock
24	Loughlin
5	Scales
3	Bradley
2	Tomlinson
22	McDermott
25	Lowes
27	Reihana
23	Dwyer
13	Nickle
26	McNamara

Subs
15	Christie
12	Medley
19	Hogue
11	Donougher
16	Jowitt
18	Knox
	Simpson (no number)

Tries: Graham (22,27), Scales (32,60),
Tomlinson (25), Peacock (42), Lowes (47)
Goals: McNamara 2, Cook 2
Sin-bin: Loughlin (37), Bradley (70)

KEIGHLEY: Mark Gamson, Andy Eyres, Matt Foster, Simon Irving, Keith Dixon, Daryl Powell, Chris Robinson, Steve Hall, Phil Cantillon, Grant Doorey, Darren Fleary, Lafaele Filipo, Sonny Whakarau. Subs: Paul Owen, Alex Cane, Marlon Billy, Jason Bradshaw, Simon Wray, Andy Senior

Tries: Dixon (2), Foster (13), Irvine (68), Cantillon (75)
Goals: Irving 2
Sin-bin: Robinson (59), Doorey (72)

Half-time: 20-8
Referee: Russell Smith
Attendance: 7,710

APPENDIX VII - PLAYER SUMMARY

PLAYER	SUPER LEAGUE A(S)	T	G(FG)	PTS	CHALLENGE CUP A(S)	T	G(FG)	PTS	WORLD CLUB A(S)	T	G(FG)	PTS	PREMIERSHIP A(S)	T	G(FG)	PTS	TOTALS A(S)	T	G(FG)	PTS
Paul Anderson	10(7)	3	0	12	0	0	0	0	1(5)	0	0	0	0	0	0	0	11(12)	3	0	12
Graeme Bradley	19	8	0	32	5	5	0	20	7	0	0	0	0	0	0	0	31	13	0	52
Matt Calland	10(4)	7	0	28	0	0	0	0	6(1)	1	0	4	1(1)	0	0	0	17(6)	8	0	32
Paul Cook	6(2)	3	11	34	3(2)	3	4	20	0	0	0	0	0	0	0	0	9(4)	6	15	54
Gary Christie	2(2)	1	0	4	0	0	0	0	0	0	0	0	0	0	0	0	2(2)	1	0	4
Kevin Crouthers	1(1)	1	0	4	0	0	0	0	1(1)	0	0	0	0	0	0	0	2(2)	1	0	4
Jeremy Donougher	3(3)	0	0	0	0	0	0	0	4(1)	0	0	0	0	0	0	0	7(4)	0	0	0
Bernard Dwyer	11(2)	5	0	20	4	0	0	0	5	0	0	0	0	0	0	0	20(2)	5	0	20
Abi Ekoku	9	4	0	16	1	1	0	4	1	0	0	0	1	0	0	0	12	5	0	20
Mike Forshaw	11(2)	5	0	20	1	1	0	4	6(1)	2	0	8	0	0	0	0	18(3)	8	0	32
Nathan Graham	3(13)	3	0	12	1	0	0	0	2(5)	0	0	0	(1)	0	0	0	6(19)	3	0	12
Andy Hodgson	5	4	0	16	0	0	0	0	4	0	1	2	0	0	0	0	9	4	1	18
Warren Jowitt	2(3)	2	0	8	(4)	1	0	4	(2)	0	0	0	(1)	0	0	0	2(10)	3	0	12
Simon Knox	5(7)	5	0	20	(3)	0	0	0	(3)	0	0	0	0	0	0	0	5(13)	5	0	20
Paul Loughlin	19(1)	6	5	34	5	6	0	24	4(1)	1	3	10	1	0	1	2	29(2)	13	9	70
James Lowes	22	13	0	52	5	2	0	8	5	2	0	8	1	0	0	0	33	17	0	68
Brian McDermott	14(2)	5	0	20	5	1	0	4	7	1	0	4	1	0	0	0	27(2)	7	0	28
Steve McNamara	21	7	98(1)	225	5	1	24	52	6	0	10	20	1	0	1	2	33	8	133(1)	299
Paul Medley	3(9)	2	0	8	(4)	1	0	4	1(2)	0	0	0	0	0	0	0	4(15)	3	0	12
Sonny Nickle	11(2)	4	0	16	4(1)	3	0	12	3(1)	1	0	4	(1)	0	0	0	18(5)	8	0	32
Robbie Paul	11(1)	9	0	36	4(1)	2	0	8	5	0	0	0	1	0	0	0	21(2)	11	0	44
Danny Peacock	18(1)	10	0	40	5	4	0	16	8	2	0	8	1	0	0	0	32(1)	16	0	64
Tahi Reihana	9(10)	0	0	0	4	0	0	0	6(1)	0	0	0	1	0	0	0	20(11)	0	0	0
Jonathan Scales	13	8	0	32	4	0	0	0	2	1	0	4	0	0	0	0	19	9	0	36
Stuart Spruce	20(1)	8	0	32	4(1)	1	0	4	6	1	0	4	1	0	0	0	31(2)	10	0	40
Glen Tomlinson	20(2)	8	0	32	3(2)	4	0	16	6	0	0	0	1	0	0	0	30(4)	12	0	48
Jeff Wittenberg	8(9)	4	0	16	0	0	0	0	(5)	0	0	0	(1)	0	0	0	8(15)	4	0	16